ACROSS A CONTINENT;
ACROSS A LIFE

A Bicycle Ride Across America into Non-retirement

KEVIN J. RYAN

Names: Ryan, Kevin J., 1957-author.

Title: Across a continent; across a life : a bicycle ride across America into non-retirement / Kevin J. Ryan.

Description: Identifiers: Subjects: Classification: Ellington, Connecticut : Kevin Ryan, [2024]

ISBN: 979-8-218-54992-3 (paperback) | LCCN: 2024923747

LCSH: Ryan, Kevin J., 1957- | Bicycle touring--United States. | Cyclists--United States--Biography. | Retirees--United States--Biography. | Cycling--United States. | United States--Description and travel. | Adventure and adventurers. | Retirement--Psychological aspects. | Self-actualization (Psychology) | Self-realization. | LCGFT: Autobiographies. | Travel writing. | True adventure stories. | BISAC: TRAVEL / Special Interest / Bicycling.

LCC: GV1045 .R93 2024 | DDC: 796.64/0973--dc23

For Joel, Ryan, Wade, Connor, Nora, Brandon, Carter,
Landon, Kerigan, Darren, Anderson, Brooklyn, Emmett, and Gwyneth

Ultimately, this book is for you.
I hope you will be encouraged to pursue your dreams and find useful lessons for
life when you read this.

Contents

PART I
Transitions, Questions, and Quest

Prologue

I lay in bed smelling smoke, unsure if the scent was real or in my imagination. It's late July 2021, and here we are—on a bicycle trip over 2,000 miles from home in this nice, if it was 1960, motel. We had ignored the smoke from wildfires across the Rockies for almost two weeks. But fourteen hours ago, it hit us square in the face.

"You can't go past Twin Bridges; the roads into Sula are all shut down to everyone except firefighters," she said, setting our lunch on the table.

I looked up, "Well, maybe there are other options; would you know?"

"I don't think so. Lots of hikers are coming off the CDT. You might be able to take the gravel road to Anaconda; it's pretty uninhabited up there, and I haven't heard any reports from that direction. Have you checked the interactive map?"

I didn't know what the interactive map was and felt too stupid to ask. I said nothing. She returned to the kitchen, and I took out my phone and Googled: "interactive wildfire map." Sure enough, the InciWeb map site appeared first in line. It showed every documented wildfire in every state, and the US maps looked like a six-year-old overrun with chickenpox. Red spots, showing out-of-control fires, were everywhere, boiling out of every range and valley. It seemed impenetrable, surrounding the town, the hotel, the very room I was now trying to sleep in.

I covered my ears, pushing my head deep into the pillow, thinking I could drown out the cacophony of voices in my head. Voices of rage, self-blame, and doubt.

When the sun pierced through the blinds—you know the ones: white turned grimy grey with dust and fried meats from the kitchenette with ends bent looking like broken fingers. I got up. Before I did anything else, I walked out to the porch and looked up into the hills. The haze was immediately beautiful and terrifying. Smoke in the mountains does that; sunrise and sunset splash the sky with pink, blue, and purple.

Later, after turning north instead of our intended southwest, I sat in the pickup's front seat listening to Gail's warm and friendly chatter. The accommodating, enterprising shuttle driver bubbled over, assuring us that shuttling from Butte to Missoula was smart.

"I've been pulling people out of these mountains for a week now, almost 24/7. All sorts of hikers doing the Continental Divide Trail, Mountain Bikers riding the Great Divide Mountain Route, and now you guys, my first cycle tourers so far."

I looked fascinated and offered a: "Huh huh, I see." My mind, however, was shouting at her – "SHUT UP, WILL YOU PLEASE JUST SHUT UP."

That same voice was screaming, "IT'S OVER, YOU IDIOT, IT'S OVER." And I believed it was.

Fires in Idaho's Lolo Wilderness shut off roads southwest of Missoula. The forecast was for increased fires, wind, and zero rain along the Clark Fork River Valley, shutting off the northwest route toward Spokane, Washington. Except for Interstate 90, it looked like roads and trails would shut down in that direction as well. I've held this dream for forty-five years, and it was over. We'd be boxing the bicycles and boarding a plane back to New England in four days.

Intellectually I knew we had accomplished a lot, that this was indeed a first-world problem, and no one really cared. But I cared, and I was devastated, angry, and filled with regret.

. . .

Regret is defined as a feeling of sadness and repentance—feeling sorry about something you've done or did not do. To be perfectly honest, it has been a recurring theme in my life when my decisions or plans fell apart or didn't work out as hoped for. It carries blame as its emotional partner.

At these times, I will eventually reach a point where I can look back and realize I have learned something. I appreciate the lessons and know there will be times in the future when I will benefit from the loss or disappointment. But in the moment, not so much.

My mind was at war with itself. I knew we'd figure out a way to get safely home. Yet, I ruminated that I could have avoided this, left earlier, rode west to east, not east to west, and maybe if I had paid more attention, I could have routed our ride away from these fires. My mental models went back and forth, round and round, all of which ended up back at self-blame.

I wondered if this was some greater message from God, fate, or the universe at large. Perhaps I had no business living out dreams and fulfilling delayed hopes. I was angry and embarrassed – at myself, because of myself. But I would never let anyone know how I was feeling right now. No way would I ever be that vulnerable and transparent.

ONE

Knowing Why

Ellington, Connecticut

Few journeys that impact your life begin neatly packaged. I have stumbled on some unintentionally and others simply because I had no choice but to do anything else. Precious few were revealed with clarity and purpose, as if to say: "Now is the time; this is the way." However, this journey to pedal across the continent revealed itself without ambiguity. It was time, and the path was clear.

It was not going to be conventional; had we planned a bicycle tour across America with precision from the Atlantic to the Pacific, it would not have started in Albany, New York, five months into a global pandemic. But it did.

———

When I was young, I had no idea what I would be, which, of course, in the American lexicon, means what you will do for a job. Looking back, I wish I had looked at those years as exploration—a journey into life itself without a need to embody a label within a certain time frame. I baked, built cabinets, and tried my hand at retail. By twenty-six, I was on the fourth venture, a machinist.

By this time, I was tired of living on the edge of financial collapse. With five young daughters and a new mortgage I could scarcely afford, I had no choice but to go to college and night school and start programming the software that moved those machines. I was surprised at how much I enjoyed this. Historically, I was not too fond of school. I was, and still am, wrapped around the soul of an artist. Logic, math, and process are not my natural tendencies. Complex problem-solving, innovative ways to express the intangible, project execution, and relating to people were my strengths. I soon realized that good design requires these aptitudes as much as linear thinking.

Time, along with that new career, changed the financial picture, and the five young daughters- Melinda, Katie, Betsy, Colleen, and Kara? They grew up, became healthy, successful women, and gave us the most wonderful grandkids.

Today, I would say I have had two full-time jobs for the past thirty years. Software development in the early 1980s led to executive positions in Fortune 500 companies, and in 1990, our church community, which was going through a leadership crisis, asked me to lead and pastor a large congregation and faith community.

I had stumbled on both roles, never purposefully choosing either, but I consider both a privilege. Journeys without intentional choice and planning. I once described this dual leadership life to a group of professional peers. Afterward, a woman approached, shaking her head; she thanked me for being so open but observed:

"Sounds awfully intense, Kevin. Insanely intense, really."

She was right. Later, I discovered she was a former marine who had survived Parris Island Boot Camp. That made her observation even more meaningful.

Approaching my mid-sixties, I was ready to turn that intensity down and also fearful of what would define life in the future. I read Suleika Jaouad's bestselling book *Between Two Kingdoms, A Memoir of a Life Interrupted*; she writes: "My fear was alive. I could smell its wet fur in the room and feel the chuffing of its breath, hot on my skin."

Jaouad's book was about facing death from a cancer diagnosis at twenty-two. I knew I wasn't facing death by retiring from two intense, satisfying walks of life. Or was I? I felt that hot breath on my skin, too.

What would fill the energy these occupations had consumed for decades?

During the last few years, I had intentionally reduced hours and commitments. I was purposeful in transitioning pastoral responsibilities to younger people with the stamina and energy to take on the care and crises of others. The years of managing a business career, listening to others' hopes and fears, and the conflict leading any organization was close to the insane intensity my Marine colleague had suggested. I understood the need and worked to control these transitions effectively, but being ready does not make the complex tranquil, and being in control does not make the difficult easy. Retirement, as we know it, isn't simple or stress-free.

The truth is I hate the American idea of retirement and inwardly bristled when someone labeled me "retired." I do not want to be who I have been and accomplish more of what I have already done. But neither did I want to sit back and fade. I wanted to establish new name tags, go on new journeys, and have different experiences.

Relinquishing responsibility is life-changing. It is disruption, not progression. Electing to give away responsibility and associated power is akin to plunging deep into self-scrutiny. I was beginning to see others make decisions that were once mine. I was no longer the voice on what and how messages get communicated; I stood aside when someone I cared about approached a different mentor for advice. I was now only a visitor in rooms I once molded by my expertise.

All of this was unfamiliar, and I did not like the inner person whose rumination was twisting in my thoughts and chest. Was I only valuable when I held a title, position, or some measure of power over another human? Was irrelevance the destiny of life's last phase?

I was surprised, given that I believed I had prepared emotionally, spiritually, and mentally as much as I had financially. This was not supposed to be happening like this, and I hid it all. I was recalcitrant in acknowledging this dilemma to myself. Saying something to someone else was out of the question. It was not going to happen.

So, why do I want to do a bicycle ride across America? The question was, how do I turn this negative voice upside down and make this ride a catalyst for an optimistic future? This bicycle ride across America would be a demarcation and point of redefinition. Saying goodbye to a great phase of life while saying hello to something different and also exceptional.

———

All extended travel is a quest. For me, this was not an expedition to find something; rather, it was a journey to let go, to put distance between what I have been and what I will become in the final third of my life. The potter Brother Thomas Bezanson said: "Life, really living, is always a willingness to end and let go and then to begin again." That sums up this trip's mission well.

I had long dreamed of a ride across the United States of America on a bicycle. In 1976, 4,000 cyclists rode across America in celebration of the nation's 200th anniversary in an event known as the Bikecentennial. I wanted to ride in 1976, but I didn't. I would now. It was a dream deferred; I would not let it be a dream denied.

This would be an excellent boundary. Like standing on the lakeshore before jumping in to slay the wounded Grendel's mother at mid-life, I would prevail. But was this possible in my mid-sixties? Have I deferred this dream too long?

Appropriately and very differently from Beowulf, I would not be alone. Cheryl and I have been together longer than apart. All the hills discussed, all the wind pushed through, all joy and trouble shouldered was ours, not only mine. I should mention that we have been touring by bicycle ourselves and with a group of friends for a decade. These trips started when Cheryl told our close friend, Warren, she'd like to take an Inn-to-Inn bicycle trip someday. He quickly responded: "We can make that happen." And he did. That first cycle tour with four couples went from Sandwich to Province-town, Massachusetts. Cycling the length of Cape Cod started this all off. We laugh when I am often credited with the beginning of our bicycle travels. The fact is, Cheryl is the source of these bicycle tours.

"Your time is limited, so don't waste it living someone else's life. Don't be trapped by dogma—which is living with the results of other people's thinking. Don't let the noise of others' opinions drown out your own inner voice. And most important, have the courage to follow your heart and intuition."

Steve Jobs

TWO

Ride Your Own Ride

The Erie Canal, New York, August 9-18, 2020

When the Covid-19 pandemic detonated, life shifted. Most experts agree it was on March 11 or 12, 2020, that the collective conscientiousness of people worldwide realized life had changed. When and how did the idea of riding the Erie Canal Trail from Albany to Buffalo, New York, during this epidemic come to our minds? It remains cloudy. Like many people worldwide, we were drained from being cooped up; this seemed doable and reasonable without being reckless or inconsiderate to others.

Albany has been New York's State Capital since 1797. The city has a long and varied history since Henry Hudson landed here in 1609, reportedly because his boats couldn't go further along the untamed river that would bear his name. Hudson believed he would find his sought-after passage to the Pacific if he found a way to get past Albany. We started the morning here at a hotel on Eagle Street, steps from the New York State Capital building. In our anxious desire to get underway, we passed up the complimentary breakfast, assuming diners or bakeries would be open in the middle of downtown. Wrong. We circled the neighborhood, trying to find something to eat. We knew it was the middle of a pandemic, but still!

Finally, we decided to head to the beginning of the Erie Canal trail, which apparently is the end because everything we found talked about riding the trail west-to-east, with Buffalo as the starting point. We planned to begin in Albany and ride east to west, ending in Buffalo, bucking convention again. This west-to-east routing perplexed me. Discovery in North America principally went east-to-west. Why did so many bicycle routes promote a west-to-east course? Was it all about prevailing winds? This directional choice would become a perpetual discussion for us in the coming months.

Breakfast? Well, eventually, a McDonalds appeared. Thankfully, it would be the only time we found it necessary to walk under the golden arches in our eventual crossing of America.

The Erie Canal Bike Path shares the Mohawk Hudson Hike Bike Trail in Albany, running north to the confluence of the Mohawk and Hudson Rivers. Riding north alongside the Hudson, we arrived at Hudson Avenue Park in Troy and soon turned left, paralleling the Mohawk River, which forms the backbone of the eastern section of the Erie Canal.

The Mohawk River shapes the only passage through the Appalachian Mountains range north of Alabama. Native Americans, the earliest Dutch explorers, and European settlers' migration west found this valley a realistic option for moving from the eastern coastal regions to the western lakes, rivers, and plains. Early paths became horse trails, wagon roads, canals, and railroads. Today, it is the corridor for America's longest highway, Interstate 90.

Traveling over 3,000 miles, I-90 connects the seaport cities of Boston and Seattle. This hallway into America's history and heartland would be our companion for the next 360 miles. Little did we know that it would also be our companion for over 2,500 miles of our traverse across the continent in a few months. We would weave back and forth, over, on the shoulder of, and under this asphalt ribbon like the laces of a boot. In Kellogg, Idaho, we would continue southwest to the Columbia River, and I-90 would turn northwest to Seattle.

We turned left out of Troy, pedaling toward Schenectady. At the corner of Erie Blvd and Green Street in a Mobile convenience station parking lot, we had our first flat tire. Flats are never convenient, but in a gas station parking lot, in a rough neighborhood, in one of New York State's top crime-ridden cities, they were anxiety-provoking. We nervously changed the tire and moved on, weaving with the heavy traffic's ebb and flow.

Relieved, we found the bicycle trail again and headed alongside the Mohawk to Amsterdam, our destination for the night. We were doing well, but I had a nagging thought: We are less than four hours from home; how would we handle flats if we were thousands of miles away, in unfamiliar places, nowhere close to people we knew or help to call? I kept my thoughts to myself, not realizing how prophetic this scenario would be.

The Canal Bike Trail intermittently utilizes the paved road, specifically NY State Route 5, also labeled New York's Bicycle Route 5. This state treats cyclists well, and when the Erie Canal Trail uses this road, it becomes a welcome diversity in surface and riding experience. We were to learn how paramount good roads would become to our daily happiness quotient

As we entered the borders of Amsterdam, Lock-10 was on our right. The locks are in exceptional condition, painted white, blue, and gold. Locks are often staffed with friendly lock tenders who welcome you, answer questions, and keep the surrounding grounds in park-like condition. Camping is allowed at these sites, and although we did not camp on any part of the trail, it makes an excellent option for cyclists.

These were the early days of the pandemic, and not only was the trail sparsely cycled, lodges and hotels were nearly empty of guests. We sometimes found ourselves in the only occupied room on the entire hotel floor. The Amsterdam Castle, which has a history dating back to the mid-1700s, was our first overnight stay. They were not serving food, and, as far as we could tell, there was only one other guest in the cavernous old building. It looked like a medieval mansion belonging west of London, England, and was made too spooky by its vacuity.

Our next two days entailed most modes of transportation this corridor has seen and most road surfaces we could encounter. After a stop at Dunkin Donuts for breakfast, we rode Route 5 west of Amsterdam again and found ourselves on an excellent road with good, wide shoulders. When we left Fultonville, we were back on the Erie Canal Trail proper and riding various surfaces. Double track, hardpacked dirt, asphalt, and crushed stone surfaces were all on the day's agenda, and only single track, basically a walking path through the overgrowth, was left for us to pedal through.

We shared the day with walkers, runners, other cyclists, boats heading to the Mississippi or Hudson rivers, trains carrying people, goods, and livestock, and local car traffic on Route 5. We waved to truckers heading as far as Interstate 90 would take them. It was a ride along a micro-environment of America's transport systems, along its historic and current infrastructures.

I pondered how many times I had ridden I-90. The first time was in my preteens to visit WWII friends of my parents in Willoughby, Ohio. Then, in 1969, for my brother's wedding, again in 1972 on a month-long cross-country drive at fifteen years old, and since then, often to visit family and friends in Ohio, Illinois, and beyond.

But in all our trips through here, I did not appreciate this valley's importance and permanence. Riding at ten miles per hour, I realized how impactful it is to know a place, its past, its why, and how it was shaped. It is true with places; it is true with people; it is true with yourself. It is effortless to pass by and skim the surface. That person and place has a history and a reason for being. I squandered an opportunity to know people or a place on a deeper level each time I floated past without pause.

A beginning lends itself to bustle at the expense of emotional, intellectual, and spiritual alertness. We can, at times, perceive activity or busyness as meaningful progress. I've been especially prone to rushing at the start of something, and the cost was an inability to see beauty or experience flashes of thrill.

As we rode into Little Falls, I was aware enough of this lesson to spend time marveling at the engineering beauty of Lock-17. This largest of the canal's locks will raise or lower a vessel more than forty feet to navigate the waterfalls in this area. We could see those falls and locks from the window of the inn where we stayed. Once again, I thought how often I had simply zoomed past this beautiful little town on my way to—wherever it was I was going.

———

After an overnight in a tired and dark Victorian B&B on Utica's Genesee Street, we awoke to a forecast for heat in the nineties over the next two days. We were about to learn lessons that would prove essential for the entire journey: watch what's going on around you, leave early, know when to push and when to be patient.

Heat is like the bad teacher, professor, or boss you've had at various times in life. Like the intolerable heat of summer, unpleasant people are unavoidable. Just like hot days rob your ride of joy, so does the inescapable person of power who is destructive. It is good to remember neither heat nor a contrary person can beat you down, make you give up, or prevent you from learning. We absorbed many valuable lessons for our ride in the heat by outsmarting, overcoming, and waiting out the adversary.

We completed our miles early before the temperature was too intense during these days. Sometimes, we pushed past it, pedaling on even when it was too hot, trying to be tougher than the fatigue that temperatures in the nineties triggered. To do this required us to visualize what was ahead. We anticipated a rest in the shade, being refreshed by a swim in a cool brook or a cold drink in an air-conditioned room. Such vision gives hope, and hope is a force multiplier. Negativity drains, reduces, and makes you small. Hope swells and strengthens to deliver mental toughness, faith in the journey, and good things expected for the near future.

> "Hope" is the thing with feathers -
> That perches in the soul -
> And sings the tune without the words -
> And never stops - at all —
>
> Emily Dickinson

Sometimes, we would wait out the heat, knowing that we only had to endure it just one day longer when it cooled down. The enduring "just one day longer" idea proved to be invaluable throughout all sections of the ride. It pushed us past the urge to give up.

———

Another important lesson we absorbed these days was knowing when to stop. Leaving Utica with the expectation of riding fifty-eight miles to Syracuse, we had to adapt. The temperature reached the mid-nineties, and going fifty-eight miles was unwise. We stopped in Rome after only sixteen miles and enjoyed the comfort of a Hampton Inn. The clerk at the desk suggested a local eatery called CJ's across the street for supper. Still, Cheryl opted to stay in the air-conditioned room with one of her favorite hotel options, Stouffer's microwave lasagna. I walked to CJ's.

CJ's is a small, nondescript, burnt sienna-colored building that looked like it was once a storage shed. Walk inside, though, and it has the atmosphere of an Irish pub: a polished walnut bar, mirror behind the stacked multi-colored liquor bottles, indirect lighting, and local clientele sitting and bantering with the owner. It made me think of the pubs we ate in on a 2018 bicycle tour of West Ireland's Dingle Peninsula. The sounds of the locals stirred memories of comradeship and past bike trips with good friends.

I've learned that the bar is the best place to sit in a joint like this when eating solo. You will be integrated into the conversations. You will not eat alone. CJ's proved itself to be the friendly place I guessed it was. I was welcomed into the craic, and I answered questions about who I was, why I was in Rome, and about our bicycle trip. As a bonus, I got homegrown advice and opinions on the Erie Canal. It was a great meal and environment; everything you want to experience when traveling by bicycle.

————

Overnight, the temperatures moderated, and our ride into Syracuse was gentle and short, allowing us time to take in more of the canal's locks and culture. We passed several large murals painted by artist Kelly Curry depicting life along the canal through the years. They were beautiful and informative and held a humorous but relevant look into the past. Canal Law #169 read in part:

THE CANAL LAW

#169 Speed and meeting of boats and preference in passing

- No float shall move in any canal faster than at the rate of four miles an hour without a permission in writing from the superintendent of public works…
- The Master of a float meeting another float, shall turn to the right, so as to be wholly on the right side of the center of the canal.

Expectations today on the canal are similar. They impose safety and encourage the quiet reflection afforded to travelers on foot, bicycle, and recreational boat.

You have time to reflect while riding a bicycle. I had to think how often I have held rigidly to schedules—and ideas. Was the importance and productivity at the loss of serendipity worth it? Had I adhered to deluded thinking in a single-minded pursuit of being right? Being unyielding, did I lose an opportunity to learn from or make a meaningful connection with another person because I hurriedly needed to get somewhere or hold on to my bias?

————

Leaving Syracuse, we came to the Melo Velo Bicycle Shop and Café, appropriately on Canal Street. It was too late for breakfast, too soon for lunch. Melo Velo is in an old brick building; the facade is painted bright kelly green with orange-red side walls. The front entrance is ramped for wheeling bikes quickly into the shop. A side door along the alley gives access to the café to order a latte or sandwich. The alleyway also serves as an outdoor seating area that belonged as much in the narrow backstreets of an Italian hill town as it did here. The place bustled with customers lined up for chains, croissants, or both. The staff was expectedly pierced, tattooed, friendly, and, yep, mellow. Bike touring is about seeing the world at ten miles per hour and savoring the simple every day, so it was a good idea to stop at Melo Velo and wait until lunchtime. We watched an ordinary morning unfold in Syracuse, New York.

Sipping my coffee, I watched a workman across the street raise an aluminum ladder against a utility pole. He was there to check cable or internet connections; a seasoned electrician would not be climbing a metal ladder leaning against those high-voltage wires for support. But there he was. I posted the picture on Instagram, and a surgeon friend almost immediately posted a reply with an eye-covering emoji, commenting: "These are the ones I see in the trauma bay."

———

The afternoon roll to Weedsport was a warm and gentle ride past locks, where we watched a small craft heading east go "down lock" toward the Hudson. I am mesmerized by this process and could watch it for hours. The coordination between captain and lock keeper, the skill in navigating the small space, and packing multiple boats together have creative tension. The keeper moves from one end to the other while the old machinery turns slowly to manage water, craft, and gate in an intricately choreographed dance. Poetry, craft, engineering, science—all at once.

Soon, we were in Fairport, a lovely canal town about ten miles east of downtown Rochester. It is a thriving community of homes, restaurants, shops, and places for boaters traveling the canal to stop. It is picturesque and upscale and, I would guess, a superb place for the residents of greater Rochester to live and play.

Fairport is also the site of one of the seventeen lift bridges along the canal. Most drawbridges I'm familiar with split in the middle, raising two sections of roadway forty-five degrees or more, enabling boats to pass through. But these canal bridges lift the entire section of the road vertically in one piece. They are charming and add to the ambiance of these villages. One side has a narrow tower that looks like the corner tower of a medieval castle. The bridge tender sits in the tower and lifts and lowers the bridge section for boats to pass below. These lifting bridges are most often located from the towpath section of the canal to the town itself. You can't stay on the bridge as it lifts, but I did fantasize about it. This single-span lift system also limits clearance to the fifteen- to twenty-foot height at which the structure rises. That limit requires sailing vessels passing through the Erie Canal system to take down their masts and strap them horizontally atop the deck. We saw numerous sailing vessels rigged this way on their way to the Great Lakes or the Atlantic.

Unfortunately, this pretty village was the site of an accident that might have ended our trip. We arrived in Fairport the morning after overnight rain. Entering the town, we looked for a coffee shop for breakfast, and after crossing the lift bridge, the cobblestone streets were wet with numerous shallow puddles we rode through without concern. One, however, was camouflaging a deep pothole. When Cheryl hit that abyss, she stopped immediately without warning. She went into the front of the bike, the shifter section of her handlebars colliding with her abdomen, and she twisted and fell hard onto the stones.

I heard a cry of pain and a clang of metal against rock. I stopped, dropped my bike, and ran to her. A couple walking by ran and helped as well. Cheryl, the wind knocked out of her, and holding back tears, she was on the ground and slow to get up. At that moment, we both wondered if our trip was over. Not knowing how badly she was hurt, I picked up the bike; Cheryl checked herself out, and with nothing broken, she, with unwarranted embarrassment, spoke fast to the couple.

"I'm fine, fine, thank you." Voice quivering.

"Can you walk?" I asked.

"Can we get you some help?" the couple inquired.

"No, no. I'm okay, really. I need to rest a bit," she replied, gingerly making her way to the sidewalk.

We thanked the couple profusely while assuring them it was okay. Frankly, I was shaken and suggested we stop here for a day even though it was early morning. I am uncertain how long we sat there or waited before continuing. Cheryl didn't break any bones but was badly bruised, with bruises on her stomach and hip turning red and purple quickly. We talked about going home by Amtrak or calling someone to pick us up, but she wanted to keep going, and we did. Although this was not a major catastrophe, it took the injuries over six months to completely heal, and a year later, they were still discolored.

An event like this leaves you unnerved, hesitant, and insecure. When I am bursting with self-doubt and worry, I do not feel good about starting something significant or pressing on with something initiated. These are the times I have withdrawn or behaved in ways to keep other people at arm's length emotionally. I'm vulnerable; we are all vulnerable when hurt physically or emotionally, and those times are hard for me to keep my chin up and press on.

Yet, one of the features of adventure travel, great or small, is that you put yourself in positions of insecurity when there is no way out except to push on and go forward. It's too far to backpedal; there is no easy exit to some comfortable place. This quality is true of travel adventures and some relationships—no exodus, no backpedaling, just forward.

As with many difficulties, this had a benefit. We learned lessons such as paying attention all the time, not assuming things based on what you see on the surface, and persevering. Excuses to stop, turn around, or give up are plentiful. Pushing past the excuses is where we reap the benefit of difficulty. I'm convinced that the many miles we would ride in the future were safer because of the education gained from this jarring accident.

———

Fairport began our favorite part of the Erie Canal Heritage Trail. From this point to the Niagara River, we found the most pleasant trail surface, the prettiest waters, the most vibrant towns, and the most northern point of our ride. We were unsettled, and Cheryl was hurting, but our last miles on this trail would be the best.

The Erie Canal and the Canal Trail traverse the south side of Rochester, crossing the Genesee River at Genesee Valley Park. The Erie Canal does not provide access to Lake Ontario, a few short miles north of the waterway. Connecting to Lake Ontario would have necessitated a way around Niagara Falls. To keep progressing west, canal designers needed to connect to the Niagara River below Niagara Falls, providing passage into Lake Erie and eventually the Mississippi River.

We enjoyed the company of five boats matching our speed and motoring parallel to us. Our tires crunching over the gravel and boat motors humming through the water harmonized in a background tune. The almost-pleasant sound was a backdrop to the gentle hills, fields, and farmlands framed by the bluest waters of the canal and sky overhead. I suspect the higher boat traffic was due to sailors who traveled from the Great Lakes up the canal as far as Rochester and then turned around back to the Great Lakes. This stretch of canal, almost a hundred miles long, would only have the locks at Lockport to navigate, providing access to numerous towns along the wide waterway.

The "port" suffix often appeared on villages along this canal section: Gasport, Middleport, Brockport, and Spencerport did not have locks but wanted the floats of former times to stop, viewing the village as a "port" for rest and commerce. Today, these towns are quaint stops for recreational boating, hiking, and cycling travelers. Their atmosphere is welcoming and filled with information on enjoying the reconstituted alleys of water and land. They still offer rest and invite commerce, as the entire canal system has done for over a hundred years.

We were enjoying a break and snack at a canal-side park east of Brockport when a well-maintained small yacht pulled in to wait for the lift bridge. Visiting with the woman aboard, I learned she and her husband live on this boat year-round on Lake Michigan, moored to the docks in downtown Chicago. They were on their way to Shelter Island, New York, to spend a month before heading south to Florida. Eventually, they would travel back to Lake Michigan via the Gulf Coast, up the Mississippi and Illinois rivers. Known as The Great Loop, this continuous waterway circumnavigating the eastern third of the United States is over 6,000 miles. The Great Loop is to boaters what a TransAmerica bike ride is to cyclists or an Appalachian Trail thru-hike is to backpackers.

Arriving in Brockport for the night, we started to feel the pull the end of trips like this create. These are ambiguous emotions of being ready to head home and wishing we weren't yet. This paradox of feelings is probably a sign of a successful cycle tour, assisted in part by the gorgeous weather we rode in.

However, the weather changed as we rode under the carport at the Hampton Inn. It looked stormy with threatening rain, but I went to Wegman's Supermarket across the street and got our supper anyway. The walk was about a quarter of a mile, and as I returned to the hotel with a bag of roasted chicken and salty snacks, a late summer downpour opened overhead with an explosion of thunder and a deluge of water. I was so soaking wet, I didn't even run, just walked in the rain to the hotel where a soak in the hot tub and a swim in the pool would refresh my weary, wet body before supper and a long night's sleep.

―――――

We left early for Lockport feeling restored and elated at the knowledge that we had ridden our most extended bicycle tour. We had pushed past a bad accident without bailing, proved flexible enough to stop when needed, replanned enroute, and did not let a global pandemic keep us home. All good headway toward an even longer ride in the future.

Entering Lockport, we advanced on the Lockport Locks, technically locks 34 and 35 of the New York Lock System. These magnificent works of engineering artistry are the last set of locks on the canal if you travel west and the first if east. They were built in 1918 during a canal enlargement and widening project to replace a flight of five locks constructed in 1838. Two locks to navigate the almost fifty feet to raise or lower boats is a better experience for the movement of commerce or vacationers than the time and activity of five. Amazingly, these locks continue to be controlled by motors and cogs installed in 1918 and maintained today with diligent care.

Approaching Tonawanda, the Erie Canal trail interweaves with Tonawanda Creek Road. We turned left at the bank of the Niagara River and pedaled ten miles to Canalside in Buffalo, the end of our tour. It was a beautiful day as we entered the city alongside US Navy vessels parked as tourist destinations reminding us that the Navy protects the inland seas of the Great Lakes as it does the world's oceans.

———

During these last miles, the idea of cycling from Boston to Albany came to mind. I had this notion while cycling a well-maintained crushed stone surface on the path with the blue canal on our left and open grass fields on our right. It suddenly hit me: we were going to complete this 400-mile trip. Now, if we cycled from Boston Harbor to the Hudson River in Albany, we would connect the Atlantic Ocean to the Niagara River, just like the canal was designed to do.

It's indistinct in my memory today if I was thinking then of traveling further west from Buffalo. I had begun to consider traveling cross-country the following summer. I had a small blue and orange yarn bracelet attached to the brake cables that Brooklyn, my then-seven-year-old granddaughter, had woven for me a few weeks earlier on our family vacation. I told her I would attach it there and carry it with me next summer to the Pacific Ocean. Yet, I cannot say when the idea manifested itself—to connect this ride with the Atlantic so that I could join them to the Pacific across the entire country.

We rented a pickup truck in downtown Buffalo and rode back to Albany in under five hours; it had taken us nine days to cycle. But during that ride, we made the plan. The next step was to find a ride with our bikes to Boston in a few weeks and begin a journey that would engulf over 3,800 miles next summer. If we did that, it would not be a direct line, not a point-to-point ride. Hikers talk about hiking your own hike. Walk your pace, your daily distance, and your maximum height when climbing. Our ride wouldn't be linear, but it would be complete and our own.

A bicycle ride across the American continent permits choosing how to handle both the suitable and the contrary. People who consider traveling for long periods may believe a journey like that will give answers to big life questions. Hiking the Appalachian or Pacific Crest Trail, walking the Camino de Santiago, or cycling across America is so consuming it may cause you to think it will transform you miraculously. I want this journey to give us a viewpoint to learn, grow, and expand rather than transform us. Processing who you've been before a journey and pondering who you will be after its completion becomes an accumulation of experiences, not a "struck down on the Damascus Road" transformation.

PART II
Connecting Dots

THREE

Eliminating Hesitancy

D Street, Boston, Massachusetts, September 2020

It's interesting how much thought you can put into where to start a long journey. We could have started the next part of this ride in a different spot, such as Connecticut's Hammonasset State Park, Point-o-Woods in East Lyme, New York Harbor, or riding through Bryant Park and Rockefeller Center. Each of these settings has meaning in our lives.

D Street, Boston, sits less than a quarter of a mile southwest from the corner of D Street and Summer Ave. We had lived on the top floor of an apartment building here for sixteen months in 2015 and 2016. We loved living here while I was working for McGraw-Hill Education. Sixty-year-olds living in a city overrun with college-age people can make you feel both invincible and invisible. Wherever you go, you are the oldest person, politely ignored for the most part. Boston is a city of revered history and future progress. It birthed democratic, computer, and biotech revolutions. It also opened our eyes to the possibilities of thinking differently, giving us energy and a fresh perspective, and was the place we experienced one of life's most inventive and cathartic times. We would start here.

It was a bright and brisk New England September morning ride to Pleasant Bay for the ceremonial dip of our tires into the Atlantic. The belief that someday, before a year was up, I would dip my front tire into the Pacific Ocean felt enormously unreachable. You can hear the tentative hope as well as the voice of doubt in my Instagram post from that day when I wrote: "… we stopped to dip back tires in the Atlantic - Who knows where the fronts will take a dip in the coming year."

Dreams are too often left unattended. To live a dream, you must commit and then take an action. At some point, you must stop being hesitant. Without hesitation, we rode to Castle Island Beach and dipped our back tires into the Atlantic. Doing anything else would be giving in to fear.

Until one is committed, there is hesitancy, the chance to draw back, always ineffectiveness. Concerning all acts of initiative and creation, there is one elementary truth the ignorance of which kills countless ideas and splendid plans: that the moment one definitely commits oneself, then providence moves too.

All sorts of things occur to help one that would never otherwise have occurred. A whole stream of events issues from the decision, raising in one's favour all manner of unforeseen incidents, meetings and material assistance which no man could have dreamed would have come his way.

Whatever you can do or dream you can, begin it. Boldness has genius, power and magic in it. Begin it now.

William Hutchison Murray, *The Scottish Himalayan Expedition*

We left "Southie," as Boston's South end is known to locals, traversed downtown and weaved towards the North end, Boston's oldest section.

———

The North End of this colonial city is one of the most remarkable places in America. It has been a merry-go-round of immigrant neighborhoods since the 1630s. This less than half-mile square section is home to some of American history's most influential. Thomas Hutchinson, the loyalist Governor who presided over the city as the revolt of American merchants and farmers escalated into the War of Independence, lived in a house yards from the front door of the English silversmith Paul Revere. Across the street was the home of the lace curtain future Mayor John F. Fitzgerald of Boston whose daughter Rose would one day give birth to America's first Roman Catholic President, John Fitzgerald Kennedy.

As the Irish left for the more upscale South End, Jewish immigrants skilled in the trades needed for Boston's burgeoning textile factories took their place in the tenement housing around North Square, Hanover, and Cooper Streets. They built synagogues to join the churches of Puritans and Protestants. Of course, these transitions were never turnkey. At any one time, the cobbled streets of this enclave would be walked concurrently by English and Irish, Eastern European Jews and Russian laborers, and eventually Portuguese and Italians. By the 1920s, Sicilian and Italian merchants and tradespeople made up 90% of the population and owned over half of the property of the North End.

It was this group of Italians that gave the North End its lasting identity. From three friends who started the Prince Spaghetti Empire in 1912 to Nick Verano, who today runs some of the area's most notable Italian restaurants, Boston's Little Italy and the North End are synonymous with the best Italian products, pasta, and pastry this side of Tuscany.

———

Cycling through my mind as I rode were questions of direction. Asking again, why is the default direction to cycle across America west to east? If we are to ride across America, can I pick up in Buffalo, New York, next spring, or must I start here next summer since it will be seven or eight months between this ride and a start in Buffalo? Would that be considered a legitimate ride across the country or not? Is it acceptable if I complete the whole thing in under twelve months?

I will ponder this and other questions of legitimacy and direction for months. Today, it is reasonable to follow America's history and migration, which was decidedly east to west. Cycling west to east was incongruous in my thinking.

Conventional reasoning would say go with the prevailing winds; that's the way a cyclist should complete a ride across America. I've never been good at doing things the conventional way. From an education path that had me finish a college degree at fifty-eight instead of twenty-two to living in different cities simultaneously, I am most intellectually, emotionally, and spiritually engaged when I elude convention and find an individual pathway. Or at least a path that is my own.

Riding in segments over eight months instead of point-to-point over eight weeks begs disapproval, misgivings of legitimacy, and minimization of our plan, effort, and, eventually, our accomplishment. But we are not trying to gain acceptance. We are trying to accomplish goals that fit who we are, our life now, how we want to ride, and when it is feasible for us. Focusing on a measurement from others would more than likely derail our satisfaction or our achievement. This need to avoid crowd approval to live a joy-filled life is germane in cycling a continent or living a life. To my chagrin, facing the disapproval or, conversely, the approval of others has always been way too motivating or deflating. It's a plague on emotional well-being. For those of us who are conditioned this way, worrying about what others think occupies too much mind and heart space. It has roots somewhere in life; mine went back to my only sibling, a brother ten years older.

My earliest memories are filled with his presence. He doted on me, let me be around him and his friends, and I idolized him. His was the primary approval I wanted, and I received it uninterrupted and without condition. Until it crashed like a building demolished with carefully placed dynamite—quick, in a heap, imploding in on itself.

Terry, or T as we more often called him, left when I was nine to join the US Air Force as our father had. He was missed, and we were proud; he succeeded, becoming an air traffic controller at the now-closed Rhein-Main airfield outside of Frankfurt, Germany, an important place in the Cold War 1960s.

The cancer diagnosis came without warning in a telegram to our home. It was the precursor to months of uncertainty and trauma. Between the shock, the terrible side effects of treatment, and his bitterness at not being able to do a job he loved in civilian life, a different man came home to recover. At twelve, I expected the approving, cheerleading, and inclusive idol would be back in my life. A tyrant came to live with us instead. I didn't understand that the anger and bitterness that consumed him had nothing to do with me. I also didn't understand his side of the experience. Instead, I entered a decades-long race to try and jump high enough and through the right hoops to win that approval again. To feel the inclusion and acceptance that had been the definition of my first and best memories.

It colored me, my schooling, relationships, and career. By the time of this journey, I had moved past it, reconciled with Terry before his death, and knew intellectually and emotionally that others' approval was a slippery slope to a boring life. But, still, at times like this, those little demons of self-doubt appeared like seventeen-year locusts, burrowing up from below to raise a lot of meaningless noise and breed into other parts of life. It was the engine right now, causing my hesitancy.

———

The day was crisp and sunny, with little wind. By late morning, we had crossed the Charles River and moved quickly through

Cambridge, heading towards Concord on the Minuteman Bikeway. Residents of greater Boston recreate, exercise, and commute on this multi-use path as it passes through Bedford and Lexington. I love this type of day on a bike, moving from congested streets to the green tunnel of a well-used path. The diversity keeps you focused, engaged, interested, and relaxed.

As we passed through a section of Arlington, we learned that this enclave was the birthplace of Uncle Sam. Little did we know that Samuel "Uncle Sam" Wilson was a patriot who lived from 1766 – 1854 and was the inspiration for the man "who wants you" for service. During the War of 1812, he ran a packing plant that supplied food to US troops, and his iconic character stenciled on those barrels became the avatar for the United States from then on.

We ate lunch in Concord at Comella's Restaurant, just down the street from Monument Square, the old burial ground, and the Ralph Waldo Emerson House. It was less than a mile away from where the Old North Bridge crosses the Sudbury River where Americans took their resolute stand against British tyranny.

Today Concord is as much a bedroom community for Boston's elite as it once was a bastion of American independence. We found the village center filled with high-end art galleries, restaurants of various cuisine, and angled parking slots for the oft-sighted Audi and Mercedes Benz. Like many of Boston's colonial suburbs, Concord is scenic and cosmopolitan. A look hard to pull off but so well done in this area.

Day two started colder as we left the hotel and pedaled through downtown Westborough past the bucolic campus of the Tufts School of Veterinary Medicine. We soon passed through mill towns and observed the next chapter in America's industrial progress and immigration. These fortress-like structures, built along many New England rivers, became the employ of the next wave of immigrant stoneworkers, weavers, and carpenters.

When Fall comes to New England
The sun slants in so fine
And the air's so clear
You can almost hear the grapes grow on the vine.
The nights are sharp with starlight
And the days are cool and clean
And in the blue sky overhead
The northern geese fly south instead
And leaves are Irish Setter red
When Fall comes to New England.

Cheryl Wheeler

Soon we were entering mill town after mill town. I could hardly imagine we were in the cavernous streets of Boston's financial district twenty-four hours ago. Now, we were in the middle of small communities recapturing the factories of the industrial revolution. Today, instead of wool, financiers spin these brick monoliths into condos, apartments, retirement homes, and incubators for tech company start-ups.

We found ourselves at Clara Barton's birthplace just a few miles from Bramanville, a hamlet once known as Papermill Village. A small white cape at a nondescript intersection high on a hill between Bramanville and Oxford was the only tiny sign marking the significance of this spot. Down and up like a roller coaster we went. At just around noon, we came on a small apple orchard. Self-service, honor-system fruit stands like this are a staple in southern New England. This one delighted with cider, crisp, freshly picked apples, and a few homemade pastries—the perfect lunch.

———

By the middle of our third day, things changed. The hill towns gave way to the relics of farms that once must have been prosperous family industries but now were tired sagging buildings bordered by overgrown fields and defeated stone walls. Hills were present, but not the sharp valleys created by the streams of the Blackstone River Valley and its tributaries. It's lake territory now—small lakes with shorelines lined with cottages and short piers ready for boats, fishermen, paddleboarders, or water skiers.

We would be home today. But the question of this ride's purpose wouldn't leave my thoughts. Was this simply a nice ride from Boston to home, or was this the near completion of a dot-connecting expedition that would empower us, position us, and commit us to a longer ride? To the journey across a continent.

Riding into the driveway of our own home was a thrill. We crossed the Connecticut state border into West Stafford on a bright, sun-filled morning. Riding through the hills and roads of familiar territory provides a special joy in bicycle touring, especially when you end up in your own driveway.

———

A few days later, we pedaled out of that drive and headed to Westfield, Massachusetts. We crossed the Connecticut River on State Route 140 past the old Dexter Mill and the Windsor Canal, which once provided safe passage around the Enfield rapids. Leaving Windsor Locks, the landscape opened quickly into flat fields of harvested tobacco, corn, and hay. We headed northwest a scant three miles from the runway at Bradley International Airport. We passed houses, small businesses, and farms that merge and jumble together in the Connecticut River Valley without defined borders between houses, farms, and businesses. The ease with which this area's land use is a mishmash of all three is unique to southern New England, making this valley diverse in landscape and life.

The next day, on leaving Westfield, we climbed in elevation, and it started to rain. Quickly donning rain suits, we climbed steeply into Russell. Ninety minutes later, the rain tapered off and stopped. We would climb over 2,300 feet this day until reaching the town of Beckett. In this old New England hill town, a sign on Interstate 90 reads:

Highest Turnpike Elevation 1,724 Feet
Next Highest Elevation on I-90 Oacoma,
South Dakota 1,729 Feet

This point, or at least this sign, has been a local landmark of some celebrity. I associate it with the nearby crossing of the Appalachian Trail atop I-90 on an iron footbridge. Crossing both as an adolescent and then today is a mark of potential adventure calling to me with ideas of walking the eastern seaboard or cycling towards the central plains.

In the last twenty-four hours, we crossed the Connecticut River, reached the high point in our trip through Massachusetts, maybe until South Dakota, and intersected the AT. If this were to turn into a cross-country bicycle tour, each point would be a milestone in our ride across America.

We reached Lenox, Massachusetts, around 5 PM. Traffic was busy, and the last two miles were uphill to our night's accommodation. We were tired and expectant for tomorrow's forty-two miles to the Hudson River at the Rensselaer, New York, Amtrak Station. There, our dots connected, and we would have cycled from Boston to Buffalo over the past weeks.

With that, I was committed. We, or at least I, would pick up in the spring in Buffalo and God willing, would roll our front tires into the Pacific Ocean next summer. I had a plan; it was no longer about dreaming. Now it was about the details – the execution. And with apologies to William Blake, I told myself that execution would be the chariot of dreams.

PART III

Making Plans. Solidifying Commitments. Facing Doubts and Doubters.

FOUR

The Plan

A long-distance, multi-month bicycle tour differs from a multi-day bicycle tour in the same way a vacation does from living in a foreign country. It's more a lifestyle change than a break from your standard routine.

We had never taken a multi-month tour on a bike. Vacations, yes; lifestyle change, not so much. We had bicycled for three to ten days in the past. Cape Cod's dunes, Long Island's vineyards, and Ireland's Dingle peninsula had created memories, friendships, and pleasing ways to see a region. Yet never had we bicycled an entire country or crossed a landmass over 3,000 miles long.

I had outlined the Erie Canal trip in an MS Word table, but this was serious. This trip needed a spreadsheet – a detailed day-by-day plan laid out in color-coded rows and columns with formulas to track and accumulate miles, elevation gains and losses, links to hotels, campgrounds, and B & Bs, all at the touch of my finger on a swipe-sensitive screen.

Between October 2020 and January 2021, I collected data. I read books and blogs of other cyclists, watched YouTube videos of trips, and searched the Adventure Cycling Association (ACA) websites, magazines, and maps for information. The ACA is an organization of cyclists dedicated to inspiring and assisting travel by bicycle. The ACA began in 1976 as a loosely organized cross-country bicycle ride of about 4,000 cyclists in celebration of America's Bicentennial. It blossomed after that ride into a non-profit organization developing over 50,000 miles of mapped cycle touring routes throughout North America. I've been a member of the ACA for years, and visiting headquarters in Missoula, Montana, was part of our plans for this journey. The ACA and one of the Association's founders would have a part in making our ride safe and memorable.

I planned as the antidote for fear and uncertainty. I want to be spontaneous and experience the serendipitous when I travel. But this was different. The truth is that I was excited and terrified to embark on a cycling trip of this magnitude. I alternated between thinking I would be thrilled every day to waking up with anxiety during the night wondering what I would do if one of us got hurt on some lightly traveled Wyoming road. I envisioned being stranded for two days, out of water, and buffeted by winds and storms without shelter. Possible? Of course not. This was a cycling trip on paved roads between legitimate towns with at least dozens, if not hundreds, of vehicles plying them daily. Still, my mind would go awash with these and other perceived threats. Plans gave me a feeling of control.

By early 2021, I realized I had to decide the direction of this trip. Would we fly to Portland, Oregon, and ride from the west to the east? Or would we leave from Buffalo and head west to the Pacific Ocean? My gut told me east to west.

I finally sat down and wrote a list of reasons why:

- The idea of saving the best part of the trip (the Rockies and West Coast) for the end is more appealing. Riding west to east, I think we would get bored from Illinois to home because we've done that many times in a car, and the best of the trip would be behind us.

- Riding east to west gives you time to get into shape before you hit the mountains.
- You start the morning with the sun at your back. This is safer.
- A minor headwind of approximately 10 MPH has a cooling effect when it's hot and slows you down minimally. Well, at least manageably.
- From all the information I could find on the internet about the question of wind direction for cycling, it appeared that summer winds move in all directions, and the westerlies are weakest in the summer, strongest between the fortieth and fiftieth parallel, and slowed down by land mass.
- You get headwinds in any direction you go. Focus on time in the saddle those days and not on making miles. Get a weather app that tracks and reports wind speed and direction daily.
- We want to go east to west. Embrace it!

So, that was it. East to west, starting in Buffalo, New York, and ending somewhere near Astoria, Oregon, on the Pacific Coast.

But plans change. And they will change again and again after that. We first developed a plan that ran from Buffalo through Ontario, Canada, crossing back into the States near Detroit, crossing Michigan to either Ludington or Muskegon, and then picking up a ferry to Wisconsin. Routes would combine the Adventure Cycling maps, Google Maps bicycle option, and where we wanted to go or had reason to visit friends and points of interest.

I re-planned and re-ran mileage on my spreadsheet, watched various videos repeatedly, and altered overnight accommodations for hours. After working on this plan and spreadsheet for weeks, I finally showed Cheryl the beauty of my scheduling.

"Why are you taking us there?" she innocently asked.

"Why do you always question like that?" I retorted with a rising, irritated tone.

"I was just asking."

"No, you're telling me I should have done things differently."

"I AM NOT!" Her voice now reaching my volume.

"Look, I have a spreadsheet, color coded I might point out. It is a first pass overview, and you are asking me why I picked a specific motel in Preston, South Dakota. I don't know why; it's a place holder. Look at the colors and miles. Feel it in total, don't ask me about the information in one cell!"

"What do they mean?"

"What does what mean?"

"The colors," Cheryl said, innocently pointing at the screen.

"Oh, for crying out loud," I said, exasperated.

Now I should mention that we seldom had tension between us during our rides on the Erie Canal, Boston to Albany, or on past tours we've taken over the last decade. But now, with all the pent-up apprehension these miles and elevation numbers were promising, I was prone to snap back with bad-mannered comments that she could take over the stupid planning herself. Of course, she just wanted to know what was behind choices and wasn't questioning my obviously masterful use of miles, elevations, average wind speeds, rainfall by months, color choices, or lodging. She was curious; I was aghast anyone would doubt my elaborate well-thought-out routes. It made us both wonder how we'd react to each other on the actual ride if we were biting at each other during the planning phase.

———

Planning anxiety reminds me of new job anxiety, a mix of excited anticipation. You're sure you will be a resounding success and you have an undeniable sense that you were destined to be humiliated, destroyed, and left roadside. In this case, literally.

By early April, our plans were firm enough. We would leave Buffalo and travel on the southern shore of Lake Erie to Sandusky, Ohio, and not through Ontario, since Canada was still closed due to Covid. From there, we would take the North Fork of the Wabash Cannonball trail, cut across Michigan to Muskegon, cross on the ferry to Milwaukee, and ride straight across to Madison where our friends Brad and Cindy would join us to ride from there to La Crosse, Wisconsin.

From La Crosse, we would ride the shoulder of the Mississippi River north to Minneapolis, Minnesota. At this point, we would take a week off and fly home for the high school graduation of three grandchildren and a close friend graduating from her surgical residency.

Once back in the Twin Cities, we would pick up the ACA Parks, Peaks, and Prairies Route that runs from the center of Minneapolis through South Dakota and then to Northern Wyoming through Yellowstone National Park to West Yellowstone, Montana, for nearly 1,300 miles. In Missoula, we planned to connect to the ACA's Trans America route in West Yellowstone. Here we planned another flight east for a church conference, allowing us to rest and see family and friends before our last push to Pacific City, Oregon, via the Lewis and Clark Bicycle Trail.

It was a good plan with miles mapped out not exceeding sixty in any given day, allowing us a day off every six or seven to rest, recover, and do laundry. Flexibility was built-in, giving us time to meet airline reservations and summertime commitments without stress.

Of course, it never works like this in practice, and Robert Burns' phrase "The best-laid plans of mice and men often go awry" would ruminate through my mind, alternating with Mike Tyson's "Everyone has a plan until they get punched in the mouth." These maxims speak to the need to have a plan but be adaptable during execution. Me, all I could envision was the myriad disasters awaiting us along the roads of America's heartland.

Burns and Tyson would prove prophetic before we would wet our Schwalbe Marathon Plus tires in the saltwater of the Pacific.

We had yet to decide if Cheryl would keep riding with me after Minneapolis, and two sections were tipping it to a no. She was leaning towards flying home with her bike in the Twin Cities and rejoining me once I got closer to the Pacific. Two factors contributed: first, this was my dream. Cheryl was amazingly supportive but had no drive at this time to cycle tour for eighty to ninety days without seeing family. Second, she was riding with an e-assist conversion on her frame, not an electric bike, but one with an assist to the crankshaft. This requires a battery, of course, and getting more than fifty miles out of a charge was not assured. Camping on our ride could find us in some places without power to charge overnight.

The two sections uniting us in worry were in Wyoming: from Gillette to Buffalo and from Buffalo to Ten Sleep. Gillette to Buffalo had two possibilities. We could ride on WY Route 16 out of Gillette through Spotted Horse to Clearmont and into Buffalo, a hundred miles. We investigated shuttles for this section and even asked for advice via online forums, hinting for some kind soul to give this old couple a ride from Gillette to Ten Sleep. No takers.

Or we could cycle on the shoulder of Interstate 90 for sixty-five miles.

Riding on the interstate is legal in some US States, Wyoming being one. Still, we had never done this, and our stress meter went from a solid yellow to full-out red when thinking about pedaling next to eighteen-wheelers zooming past us at seventy-five miles per hour, the speed limit in these states.

This narrowed our option to WY Route 16. Via Google Maps Street View, I explored these hundred miles many times. It is a secluded section of the Wyoming plains, and the sole establishment for seventy-five miles appeared to be a small bar in the enclave of Spotted Horse, thirty-five miles out of Gillette. The next town, Clearmont, was forty miles further, and between them was open ranch land.

The second section causing us angst followed immediately after: Buffalo to Ten Sleep. This sixty-four-mile ride was to be our climb over the Big Horn Mountains. The first thirty-four miles requires 6,000 feet of elevation gain up to Powder River Pass, at 9,666 feet. This isolated area of mountains had little more than a few first-come, first-serve campgrounds scattered along the roadside.

The questions surrounding these thirty-four miles—less than 1% of the total—would take up a lot of space in our minds and conversations. It was here that we pondered our age, the limits of Cheryl's battery on her e-assist crankcase, and the weight of the camping gear we would need to travel those three days.

During these planning months, I took further steps to communicate my intention to friends and acquaintances. I would gently or without much fervor drop comments into the conversation.

"Oh, we're thinking of taking a bicycle trip this summer."

"Yeah, you know, pick up where we left off in Buffalo and go on from there."

"How far? Oh, to the coast of Oregon, maybe. "

People would either ignore my comment, indicating they were not listening, or worse yet, didn't believe me. Others would perk up and say something like, "Are you kidding?"

To these folks, I would engage a little.

"Well, we're going to try,"

or,

"No, it's something I've thought about doing for a long time."

"Really?

"Yeah, since, like, high school."

My conversations were mainly tentative or understated. Inside, I was excited, giddy at times, wanting to tackle this journey and the possibilities it had in my heart as a boundary between past identities and future identities and what I would do with the next third of my life.

The last third of my life.

Outwardly, I acted blasé and indifferent. I didn't want critics or doubters to add their voices to the demons of negativity already dancing in my head.

Cheryl is different; I wish I were like her. Other than our kids, she didn't care one iota what people did or did not approve of. She would state what we were planning, where we were thinking of going, how far, and how long. She offered warm transparency about the places and roads we considered cycling. Critics didn't influence her mood or anticipation. Did I say I wish I were like that?

By the second quarter of 2021, I ended professional engagements, reduced church commitments significantly, and said goodbye to the badges that labeled my life since I was twenty-seven years old. It was beyond an inflection point. It was a paradigm shift.

My hesitancy diminished, and I would openly state our intent to bicycle across America. I like to observe people and find it interesting how some of us reveal plans and intentions during the forming stage of plots. Some people keep things close to the vest, only vocalizing intentions when they are sure of them, not wanting to hear others' reactions.

Some of us need discussion, feedback, validation, and even doubters to voice either encouragement or unbelief. One Sunday afternoon in March while driving home from church, Cheryl told me a woman approached her and, looking her up and down doubtfully, said:

"You're planning to ride a bike across the country?"

"Yep, That's the plan," Cheryl replied in a chipper voice.

"You think you can make it?" And, without waiting for a reply, she turned and walked away.

I can't thank this woman enough. I heard about this conversation on the way home that day and often over the next six months. That octogenarian did me a favor I could not have paid for by questioning Cheryl's ability and determination to cycle across America. It essentially guaranteed I would have my best friend as a companion for the entire ride.

I had a different reaction to a similar conversation, and although I knew this was all in fun, it sent me into a hurricane of insecurity. I debated again with myself if I needed to start back at Boston Harbor to be legitimate.

Weeks before our departure, a friend, someone I have great respect for, approached me.

"When are you leaving?" he asked.

"About a month," I replied.

"From where?" he continued.

"We'll get a ride back to Buffalo where we finished the Erie Canal last May and head west from there."

"That's kinda cheating, isn't it, Kevin?" he asked with an undefined smile.

PART IV
Buffalo to Minneapolis

FIVE

Beginning Again

Buffalo, New York, May 11, 2021

Friendship is intangible. Yet, we speak of it as if you can see it, as if it has a physical shape. We use language as if friendship were solid, saying things like you can build it, hold on to it, make it bigger, feel it, destroy it, cherish it, find and lose it.

A man that hath friends must shew himself friendly: and there is a friend that sticketh closer than a brother.

Proverbs 18:24

It's no wonder it takes sacred scripts and poets to describe friendship. Friendship is elusive and, like happiness, is one of life's greatest possessions.

I've heard some leaders say that leaders can't or shouldn't have friends. I disagree. I have had the greatest of friends; a few are closer than a brother. They have been there in adversity, have been my advocate, told me the most challenging criticism I needed to hear, and made me a better leader – and person.

Discussions with friends clarify amorphous plans through banter and shared wisdom. Dialogue with good friends multiplies hope and conquers fear. A person who arises to this place in life is someone you can seamlessly pick up conversations with. Distance of space or time is not a constraint or interruption.

> Long Years apart—can make no
> Breach a second cannot fill—
> The absence of the Witch does not
> Invalidate the spell—
>
> The embers of a Thousand Years
> Uncovered by the Hand
> That fondled them when they were Fire
> Will stir and understand—
>
> Emily Dickinson

Good friends Warren and Bonnie had offered to drive us back to Buffalo to start this ride. We could not have asked for a better send-off than the encouraging conversation our five-hour drive to Canalside on the Niagara River gave us. We shared many things throughout about our lives, and the miles passed easily. We talked about past bike tours we'd taken together, and they shared lessons from their bicycle tour a year earlier on the East Coast Greenway from St. Stephens, Maine, to Key West, Florida.

It was May 11, 2021. Tomorrow we would leave Canalside and start pedaling to the Pacific Ocean.

I stood at the mirror on May 12th and took a picture of Cheryl and me in the reflection. We were both smiling broadly, almost laughing. I wrote in my journal next to that picture, "Don't let the grins fool you." We were nervous, and I had to admit that riding from here to Minneapolis, let alone to the Oregon coast, was daunting. I said to Cheryl through nervous laughter, "We are not making an eighty-day, 3,600-mile cross-country bicycle trip. We are only doing a forty-two mile, mostly flat ride today to Dunkirk, New York. That's all." Our version of the cliché "one day at a time."

That was a head-fake, a weak fib to distract us from the notion that I was fulfilling a dream. A delayed dream for sure, but still a dream. I titled our first social media post of the ride "A Dream Delayed is not a Dream Denied."

To be doing something that first crossed my mind forty-five years earlier was a powerful emotional blast, especially doing so with the person I shared life with over those forty-five years. We were together, departing alongside one of the world's most incredible freshwater lakes with the full intention of pedaling over 3,000 miles.

The first day was memorable for a few things. We met our first detour early in the day after leaving Buffalo Harbor State Park, approaching the Union Canal Bridge. We had to leave the bike path next to the lakeshore and jump onto NY State Route 5. As we did, I saw the sign:

BRIDGE OUT

DETOUR

I thought, "Great, ten miles in, and we're already blocked and off-route." I could see the bridge span was passable, and the dozen or so construction workers were unloading trucks to start their day. I gingerly pedaled up to the first workman and politely asked if we could cross over. He looked around, saw his boss nod his head affirmatively, and we experienced our first dose of road magic—the kindness of this construction crew. We didn't know then we would receive friendly permission from construction crews many times as we crossed America. Only once would we get a solid "no" from a construction worker the entire trip. But what a dreadful detour that would prove to be. Thankfully, it was miles and weeks away.

———

I love riding through sections of cities like the one we encountered that morning. Busy four-lane roads turned into bike trails which ended in industrial back alleys along railroad tracks lined with massive locomotives. Backstreets morphed into county roads lined with gas stations and local pizza joints.

We entered a separate nation as we rode into the Sovereign Territory of the Seneca Nations of Indians, the first of numerous Native American territories or reservations we would travel through.

Our enthusiasm waned as the wind picked up, and we donned Patagonia puff sweaters. Soon, a twenty-mile-per-hour headwind and flapping flags freshly placed for the upcoming Memorial Day celebrations snapped hard like whips urging us on.

A couple stopped and talked with us while taking a break at a Seneca Nation restaurant and convenience store. They were typical of people we would converse with: very friendly, encouraging, and wishing us safe travels. I envisioned them to be about our age, even though right then I was eighteen years old inside my head.

We also met our first dogs, a pack of five that looked and sounded like Bassett hounds. We barked our regards in return and kept moving. Fast.

Although we arrived early at our hotel in Dunkirk, we felt the miles from a challenging day of cycling. The wind that picked up before noon was relentless. I was sore, Cheryl was spent, but we were happy. I saw a sign indicating we were approaching a child's playground. No words, just a picture of two kids on a seesaw. One high in the air, the other down, ready to push off with her feet. It was a good reminder of the ups and downs we will face in life, like a headwind.

———

That wind woke up with us on day two, and when I started to digress into a grumpy bit of whining, one of my favorite quotes from James Michener came to mind:

A ship, like a human being, moves best when it is slightly athwart the wind, when it has to keep its sails tight and attend its course. Ships, like men, do poorly when the wind is directly behind, pushing them sloppily on their way so that no care is required in steering or in the management of sails; the wind seems favorable, for it blows in the direction one is heading, but actually it is destructive because it induces a relaxation in tension and skill. What is needed is a wind slightly opposed to the ship, for then tension can be maintained, and juices can flow and ideas can germinate, for ships, like men, respond to challenge.

James A. Michener, *Chesapeake*

Does the fact that I wanted this wind to do a complete 180° turn and "sloppily" push me towards day's end mean something? Does a dip in the road or a 45° turn that increases my speed, decreases my effort, and improves my attitude make me a weak captain of my two-wheeled vessel?

How much of adversity's impact is related to our attitude and the voice inside ourselves? Can we tack to utilize the contrary wind to our advantage?

Wind or not, it was a beautiful ride through wine country and

small towns. People waved as we passed by, and a pleasant convenience store clerk let us fill water bottles with ice and water at no
cost.

SIX

Everyone Has a Story

Pennsylvania and Ohio

We crossed into Pennsylvania at around 11 AM, our fourth of what we hoped to be fifteen states, just before lunch. The springtime sky was cloudless and deep azure. The grapevines, just unwrapping their tender purple leaves, were lined up in the crisp air, and between every row, mustard seed blossomed a bright yellow, framed by posts and wires as straight and taught as West Point Cadets standing at attention.

Sitting on the edge of one of these vineyards, we met Jerry. Wearing a Dallas Cowboys sweatshirt and ball cap, faded blue jeans, and well-worn sneakers, Jerry was short of stature, carried only a small backpack, and looked a bit shy as he walked along the road. I wondered if he worked tending the vineyards.

It turned out Jerry was walking and hitchhiking from Oceanside, California, to Portland, Maine. He lost his job and had a promise of work in Portland. He'd been on this trek for five weeks and gave us some amazingly accurate information about the next twenty miles of our ride, including details of a beautiful beach he had found the night before, just three miles down the road. It seemed Jerry slept overnight on the sole picnic table at this beach. It was positioned off a parking area with a pavilion-like cover and the sound of waves nearby. I thought about how cold the early morning had been for us and hoped Jerry had a decent sleeping bag in his small rucksack.

He did not. His large backpack had been stolen. He told us of other difficulties, like walking in four days of rain and how he would periodically get kicked out of parks he had to sleep in – all with aplomb. Cheryl asked if we could share lunch with Jerry, and he gladly and graciously accepted. As we parted, she turned to Jerry,

"Jerry, take this," handing him $20.

"You don't need to do that," he said, without handing it back.

"You just gave us great information about what's ahead; it's worth that and more."

"God bless," Jerry replied, stuffing the bill in his pocket.

"Saturday is my birthday, and I am hoping to make it to Portland by then. I should be able to. I have met some of the nicest truckers across the country who pick me up sometimes."

As we stood by our bikes, Jerry smiled, thanked us again sincerely, and walked east down the road while we pedaled west.

I admired Jerry's perseverance, positive attitude, and determination. I also prayed for Jerry along with expressing thankfulness for my life and the support systems around me. Never in all my career difficulties did I have to walk across the country for a job.

"Patience and perseverance have a magical effect before which difficulties disappear and obstacles vanish."

John Quincy Adams

As we pulled into Erie, Pennsylvania, the wind settled down, the temperature moved up, and my cell phone rang. Recognizing it to be a former boss and friend, Angelo, I quickly answered it.

"Wow, you're still taking my calls," he began in his very distinct New York accent.

"Always, my friend, always."

"Any interest in doing some work for us? We have some integration work with a few companies on the horizon."

"Well, let me tell you where I am and what I'm doing," I said, going on to explain a cross-country bicycle ride in the shortest of terms.

"Man, who has a better life than you?"

There was more to the conversation than that. Frankly, I was glad this call hadn't come a week earlier because my respect and appreciation for him would undoubtedly have caused me to reconsider and delay this bicycle tour again. But that dialogue stayed with me for days. Because I felt like he was right, we had a great life, it helped silence voices of doubt and a loss of self-worth which creeps into many on the cusp of retirement. It dispelled ideas that I didn't have value at sixty-four anymore. And it quieted voices of negativity that spring up in my thoughts like avatars in a computer game. At least for a while.

We met a couple in the early morning leaving Erie who asked what we started referring to as "the questions:" Where are you from? How far are you going? How far do you go each day? What made you want to do this?

We've purposefully decided never to tire of these questions. They start the most interesting and sometimes meaningful conversations. This couple gave us great data on leaving downtown Erie to avoid morning commuter traffic and enjoy the local streets. But more, they reminded us of how questions, sometimes the simplest questions, prompt reflection, open up human connections, and give us clarity of our purpose.

———

My wireless odometer had been giving me trouble over the past couple of days, and I became agitated, apparently concerned I couldn't measure myself enough. It caused me to ask, why was measuring myself so rigidly that important anyway?

I have a colleague who often asked his co-laborers, "How do you measure your success?" It was meant to provoke self-reflection, leading to genuine self-examination.

It worked for me. Still does.

We measure ourselves and each other by numbers from the beginning of our lives. How old were we when we uttered our first words and took our first steps? Grade point averages and rank in class, college SAT scores, square feet in our house, number of houses, and number of cars are phrases with implied values. How much money and income do we make or have at retirement? The illusion is that the higher, bigger, and greater we are, the better and more worth we have, and the happier we will be.

Pedaling the last miles of Pennsylvania, I switched perspectives. I tracked average speed, number of miles per day, and elevation gain. However, I was determined to focus more on experiences and have as many encounters as possible with people like Jerry and the couple in Erie. I took the odometer, turned it off, and planned to send it home soon.

———

As we passed into our fifth state (numbers again), Ohio, I continued to wrestle with this conflict, wondering if this ride was about accomplishment and measuring worth or about the intangibles that opportunity and synchronicity could give.

But the numbers mean nothing in appreciating sunshine, road conditions, waves people gave us, construction crews that saved us miles of detours, diners scattered across small towns serving regional cuisine, and the thrilling sound of a nearby train whistle.

We left our B&B in Ashtabula, Ohio, and in less than a mile, we passed five churches. All but one looked closed and forsaken. This hard-scrabble harbor town reminded me of Pittsfield, Massachusetts because it is a beautiful place heavily polluted with the carcinogen PCB. Yet, like Pittsfield, it's making a comeback with excellent restaurants and a nice art scene. It was clearly on the upswing, yet not completely gentrified.

SEVEN

Back to New England

The Western Reserve, Ohio

Today, we are traveling the Western Reserve Greenway Trail. The Western Reserve refers to the days when this section of Ohio belonged to the Commonwealth of Connecticut. Technically, this means we're back in New England, and it's every bit as beautiful.

The Connecticut Western Reserve (also known as the Western Reserve) was an area in the Northwest Territory held, sold, and distributed by the State of Connecticut in the years after the American Revolution. We found the architecture and layouts of some of the towns in the area to be so very New England-esque that it was like being transported home.

I took time at one of our breaks to Google the Connecticut Land Company. I learned that Connecticut was one of several states with land claims in the Ohio Country going back to the colonial period. However, Connecticut gave up most of its claims to the federal government so that the Northwest Territory could be created but reserved the northeast corner of the territory for itself. This area came to be known as the Connecticut Western Reserve.

The Western Reserve had two parts. The western part of the region was known as the Fire Lands. The state gave plots of land in this area to people who had lost their property in the American Revolution. The Connecticut government sold the eastern portion to the Connecticut Land Company in 1795. The $1.2 million earned through the land sale was spent on public education in Connecticut.

The Connecticut Land Company sent General Moses Cleaveland to survey the territory and lay out townships. In federal surveys, townships were thirty-six square miles. Instead, Cleaveland created townships of twenty-five square miles. One of the earliest towns established in this region was named Cleveland in his honor. It appears that "Cleveland" was originally spelled "Cleaveland," but a mistake by a mapmaker resulted in the new spelling. Many people moved into the Western Reserve because it was accessible from Lake Erie, and in those early years of settlement, many people from New England came, which may account for the New England-like architecture.

The Western Reserve Greenway is a beautiful bike path which runs about 41 miles from Ashtabula to just north of Warren, Ohio. This area was part of the Underground Railroad routes for escaped slaves seeking freedom in the North, including passage to Canada. It is another part of the rich history of this beautiful corner of Ohio.

The sun was out in full, and we shed layers as temps went up and winds died down. After lunch outside in a small-town center diner, we headed towards Cleveland.

We biked through several economic layers on our way to the largest city on Lake Erie, and I noticed a pattern emerging since leaving Buffalo. The more affluent a neighborhood is, the less friendly and more impatient the people living there are. Lower-income areas and communities living on the edge of gritty working neighborhoods have easily been the more upbeat and friendly places we've biked. We've not yet biked in the worst areas of despair and social disenfranchisement, so I cannot speak about what would happen there. But I want to see if this trend continues.

In a text, I mentioned this to someone much more experienced than I in living outside of the US, and she responded that this was true when she lived in Mexico. It's apparently a social phenomenon that exists across cultural boundaries. Perhaps those of us who have much to lose materially become overly protective of those possessions to the point of being insular, suspicious of others, or fearful without cause.

It bothers me because I am aware of my economic strata. I thought of the biblical passage from James 2:5: "Hearken, my beloved brethren, Hath not God chosen the poor of this world rich in faith, and heirs of the kingdom which he hath promised to them that love him?" It made me conscious that I am not above anyone simply because I was born into and continue to have more opportunities and access than most.

———

We met numerous people today, friendly, helpful, and encouraging, including a couple out for a ride who started asking "the questions." He worked at The Hartford Insurance Company, and before I could find out if we knew some of the same people, up rides Bill.

Bill, a steel frame aficionado, recognized my Rivendell Sam Hilborne immediately. It turned out Bill has bicycled all over the US. He validated our choice to start in May and especially praised cycling in Wisconsin and South Dakota.

"South Dakota is wonderful. It'll change your life," he said.

"Really, it doesn't look all that beautiful," I tentatively offered.

"Oh, it's nothing for scenery, but the people, they will change your life. Wonderful folks. The friendliest you'll ever meet."

———

Shortly after leaving the Cleveland waterfront and crossing the Cuyahoga River on the Detroit Superior Bridge, a cyclist in a full-blown jersey and kit of red, white, and black, matching the colors of his light-as-a-feather carbon bike, pulled up next to me.

"Where you heading?" John asked with aplomb, but not arrogance.

"Avon," I mentioned, a little surprised.

"How you getting there?" at which, the light changed and traffic required us to move with it.

"Detroit Ave.," I shouted over my shoulder as we moved through the intersection.

"You don't want to do that. Follow me," he yelled, pulling away with the green light.

So, as we approached the next major intersection, John turned left onto a residential street running south off our planned route. The road was quiet enough for us to converse as we rode.

"Detroit Ave. gets busier and less bike friendly. I can lead you back streets over to Avon through the neighborhoods."

We shared names, a condensed cycling résumé, and our plans to cross the US.

"Nice!" John concluded. "We moved here ourselves a year ago from California," at which point John pulled his phone from the holder and up to his ear.

"Leesa, I'm stopping with two friends I met on the ride today. "

A pause.

"Yep, ten minutes."

By this time, Cheryl had not only caught up with us at the stop sign, but she realized we were going to someone's home she did not know to visit with his wife, whom she had never met. She was riding through neighborhoods she'd never been in, all while completely unsure how to get to a hotel she'd never been to.

She was sure the kids would hear about us being found at the bottom of Lake Erie, the victims of Northeast Ohio's latest serial killer.

Instead, we spent a few hours at John and Leesa's, enjoying cold drinks, laughs, and friendly conversation. They moved here a year ago from Anaheim, California, where he had worked in traffic and infrastructure for the city for twenty years before retiring when Covid hit. His work included improving the roads and greenways for bicyclists throughout Anaheim and the surrounding area.

It was a classic bike touring experience. We never learned John and Leesa's last name, but I can tell you what style and brand of bike he rides, how often, his occupation, about Leesa's family back in the Philippines, and why after only a year in Cleveland, they were soon moving back to Anaheim.

We said our goodbyes and rode the short six miles to our hotel, our home for two nights, as tomorrow was a day off and church in Mansfield. We had a weekend planned with good friends, Mark and Jeannine, with whom we've traveled extensively from Peru to Mount Rainier.

—

The next day was Sunday, and we rented a car and left our hotel at 7:45 AM for Mansfield. It was our first time in church shaking hands and not wearing a mask since last March. It was nice, it felt strange, a little uncomfortable, but we weren't overly anxious. Would Covid ever be over?

These last few days had been a juxtaposition of sorts. Meeting John and Leesa followed by reconnecting with Mark and Jeannine was different yet parallel. We didn't know the first couple, and we have known the second for years. We shared good memories, joys, disappointments, shared interests, laughs, things about family, hopes for the future, and present challenges with both couples.

It made me consider how often we seem suspicious of those we don't know. In truth, when we share that which is most personal with people, we find that which is most common. After these days, I resolved to open up more to strangers and attempt to make connections regardless of who they were or where we would meet them.

EIGHT

Turning West

Goodbye Lake Erie

We left Avon, Ohio, at exactly 8 AM on a beautiful morning—warm with a thin cloud cover to ease the sun's heat. We headed north towards Historic US Route 6.

Today, we continually crisscrossed US Interstate 90, US Route 20, and now US Route 6. Shy of 3,200 miles, US 6, also known as Grand Army of the Republic Highway, runs from Provincetown, Massachusetts, to Long Beach, California. At one point in its history, it was the longest continuous highway in the United States. A stretch of US 6 from Orleans to Provincetown, Massachusetts, is one of our favorite places. Some of my earliest and fondest memories are placed along that stretch of this highway on the Cape. From my own childhood to vacations with our grandchildren, the "Outer Cape" has been one of our family anchors and constants.

I was to ponder these three roadways periodically over the next three months. It reminded me of life overall, the importance of which path to take, how history impacts the journey you are on, the companions you travel with, and who becomes a friend as you travel —roadways or life.

Today on US 6, we traveled through Vermilion, and its streets and narrow harbors would fit along the coast of Cape Cod with ease. It was also our longest day so far, at over fifty miles. I knew we would be turning away from Lake Erie soon, and in anticipation of better wind directions forecasted, flatter roads, and the knowledge that we needed to do bigger mile days, we rode hard.

It was clear this was a prosperous area still anchored in agriculture. We came upon a construction project with vast arrays of ten-foot-high greenhouses being built as far as we could see. I couldn't even guess how many acres would be under those glass fields. Cheryl recognized the sign in front as the same company that grows the thin little cucumbers we enjoy and assumed we would be consuming them someday, grown from this Ohio farmland.

Five miles before our stop for the night, we found a small local grocery store just outside of Castalia that had the same vibe as the old Lema's Market in downtown Wellfleet, Massachusetts. It really is New England in Ohio. Just as we were leaving the store, we smelled smoke, and it became evident that the four-family home next door was on fire. After prompting the cashier in the marketplace to call 911, I ran across the parking lot and started banging on windows and doors. A local neighbor opened the home's back door and screamed to see if anyone was there, but the fire was already raging too furiously for him to go up the stairs.

Fire trucks and police soon arrived and started setting up to fight the blaze when someone who was in the house and apparently had just awakened called from an upstairs window needing rescue. Fortunately, he was the only one in the house. He was able to crawl out an upstairs window on to the porch roof where firemen with a ladder were able to help the young man down unharmed. Always appreciate your local firefighters; they may save your life.

With the excitement under control, we headed to our home for the night, a cute little cabin at Crystal Rock Campground in Sandusky.

———

We started out late today, had a wonderful breakfast, but still found ourselves sore, tired, and without coffee. Today was hard. It was a beautiful day, yet we found every excuse to stop, adjust something, sip water, or simply complain.

Years ago on a hike of the Tour de Mont Blanc, our UK guides gave our group a rule: No whinging. Now, *whinging* is a British word, and if you look it up online, you find:

———

Whinge
   BRITISH
   verb
   gerund or present participle: whinging
   complain persistently and in a peevish or irritating way.

———

Ever since that trek, "no whinging" has been a motto for our travels and lives—literally and figuratively. So, in a poor British accent, we reminded each other today to stop whinging and get on with it.

Our BBQ lunch didn't help, either, but finally, a coffee at Starbucks did, just two miles before arriving at our Warmshowers hosts, Bob and Colleen in Perrysburg. Warmshowers is an online cyclist community where a host commits to provide two things: a place to put up a tent and a warm shower to clean up.

Bob and Colleen went way beyond and gave us warm chocolate chip cookies on arrival and hamburgers for supper. Bob and Colleen have done some bicycle touring themselves, and we shared stories and plans for future tours. We then retired to the little guest house they created from their two-car garage for a warm shower and an excellent night's sleep.

———

By this point, we had departed from the Adventure Cycling Route, which would have taken us north into Michigan. Instead, we turned left and headed in an almost straight line towards Chicago. We were on our own to choose our route each day, adjust as needed, and find our best roads. The maps were put away, but we had a traveler with us that I've not yet introduced. I address her as "Lady Google." You may know her by her alter ego, Google Maps.

Although we had sometimes consulted Lady Google during the ride, we would now depend on her to route us through the plains until we reached Minneapolis. I will acknowledge that Lady Google is brilliant. She can pinpoint you globally, route you in a car, train, plane, walking, or for our case, riding a bike. Her estimates are accurate, although she forgets we are riding with forty pounds or more of kit and thinks we can average twelve miles per hour instead of our nine. Her estimates of elevation gains and losses lean towards optimism. She at times reminds me of a line from a Cheryl Wheeler song: "... frequently wrong, but never in doubt."

As miles passed, her persona grew on me, and I conjured up a whole life for her beyond my iPhone. I mentioned to Cheryl one afternoon,

"Did you know that Lady Google is Lady Gaga's older sister?"

Cheryl just shook her head. I went on.

"It's true, but being in her younger sister's celebrity shadow causes her some issues." Cheryl now kicked into a higher gear and got away from me quickly. I caught up and continued.

"I think she has some anxiety and stress because of it. Think about what happened at lunch."

Earlier, I independently decided to take a 90° turn, not on her route. Lady Google had a full-fledged panic attack. As I turned left, crossing the road for a lunch stop, here's how our conversation went:

"Return to the route," Lady Google said very politely. I ignored her.

"Rerouting." I thought I detected a slight attitude in her voice at this but still ignored her.

"In 300 feet, make a U-turn."

I smiled.

"Return to the route." Now, I was convinced her voice rose about five decibels.

"Yes, dear, relax Lady, it's okay," I said under my breath, not wanting to upset her more.

"In 600 feet, turn left." Now I'm sure I can hear her gritting her teeth.

"RETURN TO THE ROUTE." She was yelling, and I hit the EXIT button while rolling my eyes.

One day, to prove my point about her insecurities, I even recorded her having one of these conniption fits as I took a side road to look at something.

But, anew each day, all was forgiven, and we started out fresh. She is really an excellent navigator and rarely gets us into much trouble. I've thought about getting a Garmin, WaHoo, or Komoot GPS device specifically made for cycling. But that'd be disloyal to Lady Google, don't you think?

Navigation and navigation techniques on a bicycle tour are as personal as cilantro is to your favorite meal. You either love the added seasoning it brings to your journey or hate its flavor. Debates rage on the best apps, maps, and methods. You can pre-load a route onto a special device like a WaHoo or use the Adventure Cycling Association Electronic Bicycle Route Navigator for your IOS or Android device or their paper maps – definitely for the purist – or just plain wing it by asking people you meet along the way for directions. Not carrying any route-finder? Definitely for the purest of the pure.

Not being conformist, we rode a hybrid of roads, Rails-To-Trails, and ACA routes. We employed some ACA paper maps and a Rails-To-Trails guidebook or two. But, even with her attitude and schoolmarm scolding of our periodic wanderings, Lady Google and her pretty reliable bicycle option became our most frequent source of course-plotting.

———

Our next day had to be long if we were going to honor a commitment I'd made to be in Lenox, Illinois, for the coming weekend. Little did we know just how long it would be. We left at 6:45 AM and picked up the southern section of the Wabash Cannonball Rail Trail.

The Wabash is a beautiful trail that carried us into downtown Whitehouse, Ohio, before 8 AM. Whitehouse is a picture-perfect town with one of the nation's most beautiful parks at its center. It also holds one of the most memorable encounters of our trip, at The Buzz Family Diner. We sat down, and our energetic, smiling waitress came to the table with coffee ready.

"Mornin' hons, what can I get ya'll?" she asked while pouring.

We ordered a large, full American breakfast, which she didn't write down. Turning back towards the kitchen, she filled coffees and chatted up the locals along the way. I questioned if we'd get what we actually ordered. We did. Placing the meals correctly in front of us, she asked,

"Where ya'll coming from?"

"Boston," Cheryl replied.

"Really, wow. That's great. To where?"

"Today, Auburn, Indiana, and eventually the West Coast."

She turned again to serve other patrons, calling them by name and now enthusiastically telling them all about our trip.

On her return, I offered with a smile, "I can tell by your accent you've lived here all your life."

"No sir, I am a southern woman who loves the North."

"That's as interesting as a bike trip west. How's that?" I asked.

"We've been here about five years. My husband was transferred for his job; we love this town and the people here."

"Nice. What's your name?"

"Theresa."

Theresa wore a grey T-shirt with an American flag on the front, a classic dark blue apron holding a receipt book and straws, and faded blue jeans. Her long brunette-streaked hair danced on her shoulders, and her smile was as large and warm as the dining room where she was working, like a small-town mayor seeking re-election.

We learned she missed her kids and grandkids a lot, that her husband was in Whitehouse to revive a problem-plagued manufacturing plant, and they, along with the whole family, planned to take a vacation soon to Utah.

Walking toward the counter and cash register with the check, Theresa put up her hand and said,

"Nope, all taken care of, ya'll have a great ride. Can I follow up on Instagram?"

I looked at her, dumbstruck.

"Yep! Someone in here wanted to pay. Can't tell ya'll who."

"Wow, Theresa, I can't say thank you enough. Please, please tell them thank you from us," I said with genuine warmth.

We exchanged Instagram handles, and as we rolled away, I thought to myself, "This is what I wanted to find. Real America filled with good people living their lives, doing their best, and showing kindness to traveling strangers." We left The Buzz filled with gratitude.

———

From there, we met a contrary wind. Although we loved Ohio's continued beauty, we put our heads down and ground out the miles.

Cheryl traveling with an e-assist on her Rivendell Bicycle has been a game-changer for us. We can bicycle together, and Cheryl is able to cover the miles and hills while still enjoying the ride. Even long ones. I've not felt ready for an e-assist myself as yet, but I will gladly do so when my time comes.

There is a "but" with e-bicycles. You need to charge the battery about every forty to fifty-five miles. In a strong headwind, that can drop to thirty-five miles before needing a charge. I'm not sure what we thought when leaving Perrysburg; maybe we weren't thinking at all. Earlier in the day in Bryan, Cheryl's battery gasped its last electronic amp of a breath and died.

We pulled into the parking lot of a large, well-kept church on the east side of Bryan and found an outdoor plug from which we borrowed some juice. Feeling a bit guilty for using their electricity, we looked for someone to call or contact to repay, if possible, but could not find anyone. After forty-five minutes, we had replenished some of the juice, and we moved on.

Not only did this cost time, but it added the weight of anxiety, as I knew we would need to stop again to charge her battery. The problem was that I didn't know how many miles forty-five minutes of a charge would get us. A full battery recharge took four or more hours, and I was certain we'd need at least one more forty-five-minute recharge to make it to Auburn, Indiana, our destination for the night.

NINE

Long Miles and Bad Roads

Indiana

After seventy-three miles, we hit the Indiana line and still had seventeen miles to go before getting to our hotel. In our state-line selfie, you can feel the lack of smiles on our faces. We were whipped, the day was getting long, the wind high, and Cheryl's battery was low once again.

Just as we were leaving the town of Butler, Indiana on US Route 6, her battery gave up the ghost—within yards of a Subway Sandwich shop.

Now, most cycle tourers will tell you Subways are a great place to eat. The food is basically fresh, can be healthy if you choose correctly, is run by locals, and has a legitimate place to sit down. Today, we hit Subway just after 5:00 PM, so it all fell into place: dinner, booth, and electricity. YESSS!!!!

We asked if we could order, sit at a booth, and charge our bike, which the young woman behind the counter numbly agreed to. Perhaps she saw the looks of desperation and despondency on our weary faces, and compassion wouldn't let her say no. Perhaps she simply didn't care; I couldn't tell which.

Back on the road, with fifteen miles to go to our Holiday Inn Express, we moved as fast as our exhausted legs would allow. Finally, after ten-plus hours "in the saddle," as darkness was closing in and 90.5 miles cycled, we closed out the day just after sunset. The night host Jacob checked us in.

"Did you hear the sirens a while ago?" he asked, handing Cheryl the room key.

"No. What happened?" she asked, looking up.

"I can't believe you didn't hear it. We had a fierce storm come through here just an hour or less ago. Tornado sirens were going off and everything. You're lucky you weren't out pedaling in that. I upgraded you to a king suite. You deserve it after your day today. It's right near the elevator so you won't need to push those bikes any further than needed," he said, still shaking his head at our ninety-plus miles.

"Thank you!" Cheryl and I exclaimed in unison.

We both realized our good fortune in that moment. We would have ridden right into that storm if we had not needed to stop at the Subway to recharge. When something like this happens, is it synchronicity? Chance? Fate? Divine intervention? I don't think it is chance, and as people of faith, the only reaction that seems appropriate is gratitude. We had our longest day, made it safely, and felt exhausted, yet strong and satisfied. We also promised not to do another ninety-mile day on this trip. Yeah, right. Little did we know.

The next day we left the Holiday Inn Express late, and after finding Starbucks closed (something we would encounter more than once in the year of a pandemic), we finally got underway at 10:30 AM.

This day brought a lot of thoughts about planning, commitments, and balancing the need to keep a schedule without it becoming a harsh taskmaster. I wondered where the line was between creative tension and placing an unhealthy level of stress on our lives. How much of that pressure cooker is self-induced and brought on by either ego or fear that someone won't like us if we say "no" to them?

At a point over the past few days, I had berated myself for saying yes to being in New Lenox by the weekend. It wasn't that I didn't want to be there. It was an opportunity to contribute to something good and to see friends we'd not seen for a year or more. We felt privileged to be able to go there. But it was coming at a cost: long days that could have been made easier by one or two days of flexibility. I had stressed over the question of if we would even make it or not, and I thought to myself I should have just declined, just said "no."

There are volumes written about mastering the skill of saying no. I knew this and figured I had failed again to grasp that simple rule of freedom and flexibility. But I also had a very real sense that together we had accomplished something important over the past four days. We had three days to complete about 180 miles to keep my commitment. A sixty-mile-per-day average felt doable. Not easy, but doable, given what we'd traveled.

The wind was southwest yet again, and although we were feeling good, we took our time getting into Nappanee for a late supper of pizza before an overnight at the Amish Inn, located on—you guessed it—US 6.

———

Our cycle from Nappanee to Valparaiso became a positive day. We rode a familiar road, Route 30, past towns we knew and towards people we cared about. It was a mix of rural farms and small towns with great ice cream shops. The sun was shining, the air was cool, not cold. The majority of our miles would be on well-maintained roads, with a twenty-mile section freshly paved, still closed to cars and trucks but easily accessible on bikes. Smooth black asphalt all to ourselves. Bicycle bliss.

That evening in Valparaiso, we had a wonderful dinner with good friends Curt and Lyla, and we shared years of memories important to our friendship and the mutually meaningful times in life. This, again, left us with hearts full of gratitude for people in our life who have made us wealthy. Curt and Lyla would also play a part in one of the most serendipitous encounters of our trip, twelve hundred miles west of here.

Leaving "Valpo," a picturesque town with old homes and neatly trimmed neighborhoods, we rode through the University of Valparaiso campus. Going north past the high school, we turned directly west on the W550N road, once again meeting the twin joy-robbers of wind and crumbling roadsides. Where are the elected officials in this state? Indiana has reached the top of our most terrible roads list so far. Cheryl was ready to write to Transportation Secretary Pete Buttigieg, suggesting that he start the President's infrastructure work in his home state.

A few miles on, we ran into a road closure. Tempted to circumvent the barriers, we first wisely asked a gentleman mowing his lawn if we could get through on bikes. He assured us we could not. Once again consulting Lady Google, we wound our way northwest to County Road 800 towards the Illinois border.

Not too long into this re-route, we looked past the signs and barriers decreeing DO NOT CROSS, and we could see the passable sidewalks continuing on the other side of the railroad tracks. As I ruminated on the possibility of crossing anyway, two Lycra-clad bicyclists lifted their bikes and carried them across and around those signs and barriers. That was enough for us. The spandex couple was kind enough to video our illicit act to send home to the kids, too.

Soon we rode on beautiful trails through northwestern Indiana and into northeast Illinois. The Oak Savanna Trail (OST) runs ten miles from Hobart to Griffith, Indiana. It is well-maintained for the neighborhoods of these nearby towns. In Hobart, we were invited to participate in a pickleball tournament in the local park right along the OST. I assured them that it would be impolite of me to win the tournament, being from out of state and all. They laughed good-naturedly, and we kept rolling.

TEN

Friends Along Great Bike Paths

Illinois

We rode 45th Street into Illinois. It was anything but bike-friendly, and it only got worse when we crossed the state line. I think Illinois wants to beat out Indiana in everything, including topping them for how bad their roads can be. What kind of thinking puts rumble strips all the way past the white line to the right? It doesn't make sense; by the time a car would hit them, it would be too late to be warned. They've driven too far off the road to have time to correct.

Rumble strips get lots of attention and discussion in bicycle touring circles. Cutting directly over or on the white line, with thirty to thirty-six inches of ridable shoulder to the right, is welcomed. But please, strips on the right side of the white shoulder line or right up to the edge of the shoulder pavement is a safety hazard for drivers and cyclists alike. They are useless.

After a few anxiety-ridden, vibrating miles, we picked up our next trail, the Thorne Creek. This trail is lovely and follows the meandering tract of Thorne Creek for over seventeen miles. We pedaled to the junction with the Old Plank Road Trail, a twenty-mile-long former railway running from Chicago's south side neigh-borhoods to the fast-growing suburbs out to Joliet, where it connects to the Illinois Michigan Canal trail system. What Illinois lacks in comfortable roads, it makes up for with its bicycle trails.

Thirteen miles from day's end, we met up with Brad and Cindy. It was our third encounter with good friends in a week. We would be staying with them for the weekend, and they would be joining us later to ride from Madison to La Crosse, Wisconsin, for four days.

After a shower and a great meal of tapas at The Dancing Marlin, we found ourselves sleeping soundly with the satisfied feeling of knowing tomorrow was a zero-mileage day of worship and friendship with a people we've known for over forty years. Life is indeed good.

———

Monday morning came early, too early. We headed out once again on the Plank Road Trail towards Joliet. It was a sunny morning, and we moved quickly and easily. Part of that ease was due to the being ten pounds lighter. Knowing we would not need our camping gear for the next ten days, we shipped tents, sleeping pads, bags, and clothes to the Marriott in Bloomington, Minnesota, just south of the Twin Cities.

I was surprised at the difference and pondered how we have reached a point in life where shedding stuff is an excellent habit to develop.

Years ago, when given a promotion, I asked my boss for advice to do my new job well. His answer has stayed with me

"How do you do this sort of thing given the number of people, large budget, multiple responsibilities?" I asked.

"Stop mowing your lawn," Dick responded, straight-faced.

"Huh?"

"Yeah! Stop mowing your lawn."

"But I like mowing my lawn," I entreated.

"Yep, me too. But you can't keep doing things that are not adding value to what you are being asked to do now. At least not until you know what you're doing in this job. Then you'll have given some tasks to others and learned how to do things you must do quickly. The problem is, then you'll be given more responsibility, more people to lead, and more fiscal obligations. At that point, you'll be looking for the next thing you're doing that you'll need to give away, have someone else do for you, or ignore. If you want to do this job well, stop mowing your lawn. If you do it well, you'll probably not mow your lawn again until you retire."

"Ah, okay?" I faltered.

The thing is, Dick was right. I hired someone to mow the lawn and never mowed it again for twenty-five years. This wasn't time management he was talking about. It was shedding--knowing what (and when) to cut out extraneous things and activities to empower you rather than encumber you.

Of course, Dick was giving me life advice more than career advice. Stop mowing the lawn became a metaphor for letting go or ignoring the things, people, habits, or thought patterns that weighed me down emotionally, spiritually, or intellectually. Bitterness, anger, bad choices, toxic relationships, and mind-numbing technology are the lawns to stop mowing for progress.

———

Shortly after exiting the Old Plank, we met Michael, who was touring east from California to New York City along Historic Route US 66. Michael was the first cross-country cyclist we'd met, and it was fun to talk about everything from gear to wind resistance. Michael did seem to complain about the wind quite a bit, maybe even more than we did. I wondered how, heading in opposite directions, we both seemed to whinge about headwinds.

After a night in St. Charles, we headed out on the Great Western Trail and into Genoa. The first twenty-five miles were excellent, and then Mister WSW wind found us again. The final twenty-eight miles were tough. Winds were twenty miles per hour with gusts higher, supercharged by the passing eighteen wheelers. At one point, I was blown off the road and tossed into a ditch. After that, we started to pull over when trucks went by rather than being pummeled to the ground.

The storms in the area passed by without drenching us, and our last miles through downtown Rockford were on crumbling roads through equally crumbling neighborhoods. Recently ranked by *US News* as one of the nation's best places to live, I saw a sad city. The exception was a three to four block downtown area on the Rock River.

Because the next day's forecast was for increasing storm and wind, we took a day off in Rockford. This would require us to do a seventy-seven-mile day into Madison, but winds were forecasted out of the east, giving us a tailwind. Though colder with rain, it was still better than the twenty-miles-per-hour headwinds. We hoped

When we were in Valparaiso, Indiana, at supper with Curt and Lyla, we discussed our reasons for riding east to west. Curt is a farmer, and he wondered aloud about the wisdom of this direction given the prevailing west wind in America.

He referenced the adage, "When the wind is blowing in the east, it's not fit for man or beast."

Remember that part about doing seventy-seven miles in the rain, cold but favorable wind? Well, it worked great for almost fifty miles. Until it didn't.

ELEVEN

Standing at the Threshold

Wisconsin And the Mississippi River

We crossed the Wisconsin border, our eighth state, dressed in down fleece jackets, hats, and gloves more fitting for February than late May. Wisconsin is fantastic bicycle territory. The roads are in great shape with wide shoulders, rumble strips placed well if they exist, and courteous people. The scenery is as if New England and Mid-state Illinois had children.

The winds were at our right shoulder, and we flew through our first forty-five miles before noon. It was cold but lovely. I imagined the tall grasses now blowing in the direction we were heading to be crowds waving us on to victory.

And then the rain hit.

And the east winds shifted north.

And our status turned from golden to grim.

We were soaked by mile sixty-one and riding in a rural area without a convenience store, gas station, or family diner to be seen. We were cold and spent, and so was Cheryl's bike battery.

I considered knocking on someone's door and asking for a dry space with an electric plug to juice up her bike, but we pedaled on and hoped the battery charge was enough. I have heard it said innumerable times: Hope is not a strategy. How true.

Her battery (the bike, not Cheryl's) died eighteen miles outside of Madison, just as we rounded a corner in front of a mammoth horse barn. Walking up the long drive, we were welcomed by one of the boarders renting space in the barn. She assured us it was fine to come and warm up. This stable was a true refuge in the storm with a heater blasting in the tack room, surrounded by the sweet smell of hay, grain, and leather. Rescue.

As mentioned earlier, Brad and Cindy were on their way to meet us for a few days touring through Wisconsin. I texted Brad to ask about picking Cheryl up. He was eleven miles away. Rescue and relief.

They arrived within twenty minutes, and Brad took his bike off his bike rack, lifted Cheryl's on it, and rode the last eighteen wet, cold, rainy miles into Madison with me. Have I mentioned the value of friendship on a bike tour?

Yes, it was miserable. And yes, we were still happy! As the adventurer, Yvonne Chouinard said: "... when everything goes wrong – that's when adventure starts."

I don't want to understate or overdramatize it. But today took us to the limit of our mental endurance. I don't know what we'd have done if that horse barn wasn't there. The only other option was to knock on that random door. And I came very close to that.

I knew there were lessons here, and I wondered what exactly they were. It was the end of May and so unseasonable that temperatures were in the thirties. Though rural, there were still people and houses close by, but I wondered what would happen if we ran into a similar situation in western South Dakota or the hills of Wyoming. There are places in the west that are far more remote, and there's no Brad eleven miles away with a car and bike rack. My anxiety about cycling in the Western states elevated as I tried to sleep that night.

———

Our first day aside, Wisconsin was to become our favorite cycling state of the entire cross-country trip. I am still determining if that is because of the wonderful roads, courteous drivers, amazing scenery, or great company we had through most of our days there. Or was it simply because, like life itself, it was the pre-midlife stage of our tour? More on that later.

Interestingly, in cycling 3,879 miles across America we had only one individual show of aggression or anger toward us, and that happened in Baraboo, Wisconsin. However, I can't say he was a Wisconsinite. As we were leaving the hotel on our third morning, a man saw us rolling our bicycles out the door, and as Brad said, "Good morning," he replied, with an angry look and expression damning us to eternal destruction. I smiled and walked past.

We quickly made it to Sauk City for another diner lunch along the Wisconsin River and continued on the Great Sauk Trail (GST). The GST parallels the Wisconsin River through the communities of Prairie du Sac and Sauk City and is built on a former Union Pacific Rail line. It was unique in that, like some of the other Wisconsin Rail Trails, it had a day-use of $5, all on the honor system.

About ten miles out of Sauk City we came upon a fascinating area. Here's the introductory description posted on the sign:

The Badger Ordnance Works was built on the terminal moraine and outwash plain of the glacier that stopped here about 12,000 years ago. This out wash plain is known as the Sauk Prairie named for the Sauk Indians that had a village of 90 homes where Sauk City is located today.

Today, it is laced with old roadways empty of buildings and returning to the raw prairie.

I would love to have been able to spend a day riding and reading the numerous signs explaining, what was in 1942, the world's largest ammunition factory to support America's WWII effort. The Badger Ordnance Works is located at the southern foot of the Baraboo

Bluffs and must have been impressive at the height of the war. I could only imagine the people, trucks, and rails moving across this plain to move explosives and munitions to the far reaches of the European and Pacific theaters. Now, almost eighty years later, it is basically a feral field growing up around narrow streets. When viewed from the bluffs, it looks like a circuit board gone dark.

———

Soon we found that the trail just petered out. Or we were lost. Lady Google sent us up the ridge line on an unused road heading to the top of the Bluffs. Something felt amiss, and we should have turned around. Which of course we didn't, assuming the signs were meant for cars, surely not for bicycles. You'd think that reading every so often "Rescue Point 1S or Rescue Point 4F" and so on would give us pause. Nope, the prospect of adding five miles to our ride if we turned around kept us keepin' on.

Until we came to a sign explaining why. It read:

ATTENTION

Ho-Chunk Nation and Reservation Lands are closed to the public at this time. Please respect all Badger Land Owners and be cognizant of closed areas and closed roads. Trespassers will be subject to civil and criminal penalties.

Well, there was no bicycle exemption, so we followed those old Badger Ammunition roadways out to RT 12, but still not over the South Bluff /Devils Nose State Natural Area. Our five-mile detour was turning into a twelve-mile circumvention of the tribal land area.

———

The next day, we left Baraboo's Clarion (misnamed) Hotel at 9 AM for a short thirty-one miles into Mauston. It was a class 1 day. There were slight winds at our back, blue skies, bright sun, and empty country roads in excellent shape with shoulders when needed. This is biking as it should be.

We soon met Dave Anderson, the superintendent of roads in Lemonweir Township, Wisconsin. He is evidently part of a group in Wisconsin that knows what they are doing. Not only is Wisconsin the prettiest state we've ridden so far, but it universally has the best roads of any state we've ridden—ever.

Kudos to Wisconsin's road superintendents. And, as painful as it is to write, this state is maybe prettier than New England. I journaled at day's end,

Wisconsin:
- Bike it when you can
- Thank all the Dave Andersons you meet
- Hope for windless days
- Sunny weather
- Bright blue skies

We stayed the night at The Lodge, a Wyoming-inspired hotel and event center built by a local entrepreneur who has a successful manufacturing, cattle, and lodging business. He was well spoken of by townsfolk and employees alike as someone who cared about people and gave back to the community. Very nice.

————

Our last eight or so miles were…tough. We stopped two and a half miles from our overnight destination for supper at a place called The Cotter Pin. According to Lady Google, the last miles were "mostly flat," as she likes to say, but sometimes she is more optimistic than factual. We were all glad to be done with those last of our totaled fifty-five miles. After a shower and a nice walk around the beautiful property, we enjoyed the proverbial sleep of the dead until we woke fresh to a crisp morning with the surrounding hills covered in morning mountain fog.

A relaxing morning started with coffee (good coffee, at that) in the garden. The Driftless hills dissipated as we watched cardinals eat their morning breakfast at a feeder just feet away. We were in the heart of the Driftless Area, sometimes called Bluff Country or the Paleozoic Plateau. It is legitimately a geological marvel. When glaciers retreated across the American plains, they somehow skirted around the area of what today are the corners of Illinois, Wisconsin, Minnesota, and Iowa. Because they did not scrape across this plateau, they did not leave glacial drift of rocks, sand, till, and water. Hence the term "driftless."

Years ago, I learned about the region while fishing with my good friend Ken, a flyfishing master who showed me the ropes of this art. A trip to the area was one of numerous fishing escapades we'd taken over the years in the American West. The Driftless is littered with small, limestone-fed, aquatic-rich streams of cold, clear water escaping the subsurface aquifers filled by the last ice age to scar the American Continent. A perfect habitat for trout.

When you are in The Driftless, you think you are in a mountainous area with hills, ridges, and valleys in all directions. You are actually in the ravines of a plateau where those rivers and streams have carved the valleys out of the high ground. The assumed mountain tops are basically the same height and flat from one to the next. It is more like erosion on a grandiose scale than mountains lifting from the surface.

Our ride through here could be described as wonderfully short, sun-filled, carless, and full of anticipation. It was a perfect day to reach the milestone of seeing the Mississippi at La Crosse.

I think there's something intrinsic in us as humans that marks boundaries with significant bodies of water. We started this trip in Boston Harbor, crossed the Charles, the Connecticut, the Hudson, the Mohawk, and rode parallel to the Erie Canal. We had the international border with Canada on our right for days as we pedaled along the Niagara River and then the southern shore of Lake Erie.

But for us, today is a major milestone and a boundary - the banks of the mighty Mississippi. The Mississippi is both a beginning and an end. It begins our track across the prairie, and it ends the safe and familiar feeling of the East where towns are close and nothing seems far away. We will cross numerous rivers, such as the Missouri, the Bitterroot, and others, but nothing else holds the mystique of this river. America's second longest river, it is the water supply for more people than the population of England, is eleven miles wide at its widest, and is recognized as the inspiration of American literature.

Reaching the Mississippi on Memorial Day added to the sweetness and sharing it with friends a bonus. Cheryl and I passed 1,500 miles pedaled, reaching its eastern shore.

———

La Crosse was the site of a major event. As discussed earlier, Cheryl was uncertain about traveling with me past Minneapolis. Of the concerns causing her hesitancy, only one remained to be resolved, and at a riverside park, she looked at me and said, "If you bring a second battery along for my bike, I'll go with you to the West Coast."

The next day, filled with gratitude and expectation, I called our bike mechanic and ordered that battery for her e-assist. I have no idea if, reading this, someone will give judgment to the validity of riding coast-to-coast with a battery-assisted bicycle. Honestly, it's not important because, for us, it empowered our continuing together as much or more than it powered her two-wheeled transport.

———

We bid farewell to Brad and Cindy in La Crosse and headed north along the Vietnam Veterans Trail, connecting us to the Great River State Trail. Once again, Wisconsin is to be credited for how much care it gives cyclists. The trailhead at the beginning of the Great River State Trail even has showers available for use. The trail itself could have been better, but it was fair overall. Trails here are surrounded by history, and the maintainers explain the area and its past. Just outside Trempealeau, we found some Hopewell burial mounds.

The Hopewell were an ancient Native American culture that inhabited vast regions of North America. Their lands extended from the Gulf of Mexico to the eastern Great Lakes, basically the entire Mississippi and Ohio River valleys. They built mounds of all sizes for burial, and today these mounds are found throughout these river regions. But as we were to learn repeatedly on this trip, names and events given to native cultures are often misrepresented and filled with contradictions. The name "Hopewell" is a case in point. The name has nothing to do with this fascinating native culture but was labeled such because the first mound discovered was on land owned by a Mordicai Hopewell in Ross County, Ohio.

The Hopewell people were a complex and vast culture of hunter-gatherers and trading communities. They flourished in these areas from approximately 200 BC to 500 AD. There is a mound in Chillicothe, Ohio, that the US Park Service manages and is under consideration or has been designated a UNESCO World Heritage Site. I've been vaguely aware of these mounds for years and always wanted to visit one. Finding a mound on this bike trail was incredible.

After our contemplations at the mound, we crossed the Mississippi and into Minnesota at Winona around 1:20 PM. Winona was our stop for the night. It was the third consecutive stellar day with the wind at our back, perfect temps, and bright sun all day.

TWELVE

Midwestern Nice

Minnesota

We left Winona in good time on Minnesota RT 61. This is part of the Mississippi River Trail, also known as MRT or US Bicycle Route 45. I know -- confusing. The MRT is a designated bicycle and walking trail that traverses the shores of the Mississippi, extending from the headwaters at Lake Itasca, Minnesota, to the mouth of the river in Venice, Louisiana.

I was loving the ride along the Mississippi, but I wondered where the commercial traffic was, having yet to see any. Alas, a barge appeared heading upstream. And the bonus was watching it pull into lock #5.

Like the Erie Canal locks, these locks are beautiful, exquisitely maintained, and well-explained. Diagrams described the locks and boats that ply this section of the Mississippi. For lunch, we pulled into the quaint downtown of Wabasha and found an Irish pub with vibes as real as a family favorite in Boston.

Not long after, we were on the shores of Lake Pepin, the largest lake on the Mississippi. It is a naturally occurring lake formed by the delta of the Chippewa River, which enters the Mississippi from Wisconsin upriver from Wabasha. The Chippewa constricts the flow of the Mississippi, forming Lake Pepin between this point and Red Wing. The recorded history of the lake goes back to the early 1700s. It is very old for this part of the country and has a long history of being a magnet for recreation; the sport of waterskiing was invented on the lake in 1922.

Lake Pepin is also home to Lake City, our stop for the night. We were early and only a mile or so from a barbershop. What good fortune, I thought. Off to Lake City Barber Shop I went where I met Mike, the owner and sole barber. We were soon joined by Joe, Mike's next customer. Mike and Joe had a lot of questions about a cross-country bike ride. Good questions.

Mike is well traveled. Years ago, he took a month-long Amtrak trip around the US, a two-month east coast drive with his daughter, and many road trips to the American West. He's been a mail carrier, restaurant owner, and now barber. And he knows how to provide value for his services -- I am pretty sure I won't need another haircut until after Labor Day. So, not only did I get value for my $16, but Cheryl was entertained for hours as she couldn't stop laughing when she saw how scalped I was.

———

Our next day was about forty-two miles to the burg of Hastings, a shorter day overall, and we encountered the town of Red Wing late in the morning. We stopped at Mandy's Coffee and Café for a brunch of sorts. Red Wing, like many of these Mississippi River towns, has a lot going for it. Clearly, people living there care, civic leaders serve the community and industry, and resources are used effectively. We in New England could learn from these folks, and I'd encourage you to visit when and if you can. The MRT has now found its way to our list of potential future bicycle tours.

———

With heat and wind forecasted for our ride into Minneapolis, we left at 7 AM the next morning for the thirty-mile ride to the Element Hotel at Minneapolis/St Paul airport. The wind once again was in our faces, and looking at the blowing flags in the area, it seemed to be higher than the predicted ten miles per hour.

At the five-mile point, we had a choice -- continue in a straight west direction into a WSW wind or turn north onto a county road. The road was gravel even though Lady Google's satellite views showed asphalt. So, we took the gravel, figuring bumps were better than headwind. That turn put the wind at our left shoulder, which made all the difference, and soon the gravel turned to a new asphalt surface. We had twenty-five miles of excellent roads with wind assist instead of resist.

It became clear we were at an inflection point in our journey across the continent. As we prepared to fly home for a week, our hearts were in two places. We anticipated going home to see family and friends with excitement, and we felt the tug to move on and not pause right now. Things were going well; we had a daily rhythm, we knew what we were doing, and our tentativeness within the early days of our ride had been replaced with confidence. We did not want to lose the palpable momentum that had replaced the apprehension.

Other times in life are like this. A new promotion causes you to focus on applying past knowledge to new challenges; you want to be at work a lot, working extended hours, and spending energy on the new opportunity. At the same time, you are needed at home to give your children or your marriage extra time and energy. Two good things at conflict in you.

But inflection points, by definition, involve changing one state into something different. The concave becomes convex. The familiar becomes strange. It is a period of change. Psychologists will tell you that human beings dislike change because it leaves us with a sense of lost control or because it leaves us doubtful and insecure about our ability to adapt to the new order.

I try to focus on the transition, the period between the current state and the new. We were at a transition in our ride, and being honest with myself, I was aware that at sixty-four years old I was a point of flux in life. I was the same age that my father was when he died after a ten-month battle with cancer. That transition had a major impact on why I was on this ride now.

My father, Jack Ryan, was a WWII Purple Heart recipient who did his duty to family, church, country, and company—pretty much in that order. He was slated to retire at sixty when the company asked him to stay on for two more years. Without hesitation, he said yes. It wasn't the extra money or prestige of a promised promotion. It was duty. He had less than sixteen months of a good retirement. His last eight months of life were painful and hard.

Those two years were a point of change for me, as well. From the time of his death, I decided that I would not delay dreams on account of obligations to institutions that would move on undisturbed once I'd exited. His death was the inflection point, and job changes, moves to various cities, travels from Peru to Europe, and the approximately 1,200 miles we'd pedaled over the past weeks are traced back to his decisions and death.

Transitions are where growth and lessons can be learned, and a week at home among the familiar and friendly would prove to be a useful passage into the vast American prairie.

PART V
Beginning Again

THIRTEEN

Shifting – More Than Gears

We had spent seven days at home to share celebrations, milestones, and reconnections, primarily the high school graduation of our grandchildren Nora, Connor, and Brandon. Graduations especially are a bridge of generations: kids want their parents, grandparents, cousins, and extended family at this point in life. They know it's meaningful but are still too young to grasp the full significance.

I remember my high school graduation well, but I don't think my grandchildren graduating now will fully appreciate this life moment for many years, just as I hadn't forty-six years ago. It's not necessarily the most significant event; college graduations, marriages, occupations started, and children of their own will all be more substantive. Yet, this is the first time they depart an institution, embark on a life milestone as an adult, and leave friends they won't see for years, some never again. It is life's first significant change for most Americans.

As they hit their first big transition, I wondered if we were in the middle of one of our last. Phrases like "retirement," "slowing down," "downsizing," and "moving to a new phase of life" were entering our conversations. For me, these phrases felt like nice ways of saying that your life is over now; time for you to head into uselessness. I was increasingly reluctant to answer questions from people such as, "What do you do?" or my absolute least favorite, "How's retirement?"

A friend approached me one day while home and asked, "So, how's the transition going?"

"Well, I think it is going well. I think those who've taken over the leadership are doing a great job; we are enjoying our trip and looking forward to what's next," I answered with a tad of caution.

"What's it like to be a nothing now?" he added with a strong sense of emotion.

I was staggered and didn't know how to respond. All I could get out was, "Is that what I am?"

He explained that he felt discarded when he turned over the leadership role in a business and moved to a comfortable but far more sedate phase of life.

I have thought a lot about this conversation since and realize he was not asking about me or my transition; he was reflecting on his own. I took this exchange as a gift, a prompt to ensure I did not simply move to sedation and ease and a shove to find a "next," whatever that next was. But it also prompted me to think about this time at home more as a reprieve from our summer job – Cycling across America. This trip and being at home had flipped my mind to where the journey was the occupation. Completing it to earn the reward was the objective. It was as if each milestone cycled was an exam passed, a promotion earned, or a bonus awarded.

———

The days at home were sunny and the company warm. We walked around the yard and marveled at how green everything was and how complete the gardens and flower beds were. We had left a mere four weeks ago, and the grasses and flowers were springing out like little birds poking their heads over the edge of the nest. Now, they were fully grown and flying with color and growth. I thought about how we don't see life changes when we look at the day-to-day. Then we see a photo or a video from just a short time ago and remark on how much we all changed.

Changes and the healing that comes from transitions in this trip continued to pile up. I recognized that more time away from here would make the September reunions and reattachments a better launching pad for whatever the future would hold. But it was time to go back on the road, and on June 14th· we flew back to Minneapolis.

———

We woke at 4:15 AM and were in the Southwest Airlines line by 5:00. It was still time-consuming and stressful to go through the serpentine queue to get boarding passes, luggage checked, handed off to TSA, queue into the pre-check line, and get to our gate so as not to miss that important A-Group.

I've come to hate flying. I really do.

By 12:30 PM, we had paid our Uber driver and stood outside Tangletown Bike Shop, located on the ground floor of the Bachman Building, an ornate brick structure on 50th Street built in 1919. We left our bikes there for service and safekeeping, and Mike, the owner, met us there on his day off. After collecting Cheryl's battery that we'd shipped to him, we packed up, paid Mike his reasonable fees, purchased chain lube and a new helmet (I had left mine at home), and headed towards Excelsior, Minnesota, twenty-nine miles west.

Tangletown is a neighborhood that has grown up without the typical Midwest practice of placing streets in grids and squares. We wove around bends and corners as we rode past city parks lined with walking paths to small lakes and gazebos where people enjoyed sunny and warm lunchtime strolls.

As we pedaled around Lake Harriet, the bike felt foreign to me, and the comfort I had developed in those first four weeks of touring seemed lost. Lake Harriet is a round lake with a walking and cycling path around the entire lake. We stopped for ice cream at the bandshell, where many of the region's teens were enjoying their summer freedom from classes.

The Bird House Inn at Excelsior was our stop for the night. Both of us were tired after the first day cycling again, and after an early supper, we were asleep well before dark. I estimated we had ridden over 1,300 miles from Buffalo and 1,700 miles from Boston, meaning somewhere near here, we had or were about to hit our halfway mark. Time and unexpected barriers would prove me way low on this estimate, but fortunately, I didn't know it as I fell asleep that night.

The Bird House, a pink Victorian home turned inn, is a block from the Lake Minnetonka Regional Trail. It is perfectly seated for bike touring. Kowalski's Market, several restaurants, and breweries are within walking distance along the streets leading to Port Park on Excelsior Bay. Our innkeeper, Amy, was delightfully helpful. She had a unique way of letting me know Minnesota was not her home. I wanted to ask about dinner and noted a Mexican place within a short walk towards the bay. As Amy walked into the living room while I was waiting for Cheryl, I said to her, "Is the Mexican place down the road a good place?"

Hesitating, Amy replied, "Well, I'm from south Texas originally."

"So, you wouldn't recommend it then?"

"Oh, no, people here love the place," she replied, deadpan.

"Okay, got it," I said, laughing.

———

The next five days were everything we hoped for, and everything we feared.

We left Excelsior around 9:30 AM, late considering we planned to ride over sixty miles this day. But the weather was excellent, and the wind was cooperative. When we connected to the North Cedar Lake Trail, the discomfort of being back on tour and feeling foreign on the bike had disappeared. Today, we would be on bike paths, including the Dakota Rail Trail and Luce Line State Trail.

Minnesota rivals Illinois for its trail system, and the New England states have much catching up to do to reach the standards set by our Midwest cousins.

The Dakota Rail Trail passes right through the middle of New Germany, Minnesota, and we were blessed to ride past the Lutheran Church right at noon. The bells were playing familiar hymns, and my allergies must have kicked in right then as my throat was tight, my eyes watered, and I couldn't say a thing.

As we rode on nondescript roads that afternoon, a man pulled up beside me in his pickup. Rolling down the window, he started asking the usual questions as we all moved forward at ten miles per hour. When I mentioned we had started in Boston, he about yelled, "I gotta pull over and talk to you guys."

He pulled ahead, jumped out of his truck without actually pulling over, and ran back to us.

"Did you say Boston, as in Massachusetts?"

"Yes. That's right," Cheryl replied. I guess it was her turn to answer questions today.

"I bike, too, around these parts anyway. But all the way across the country! That's insane."

"Well, insane, crazy, and out of your mind are the three most oft-used adjectives we hear. Once in a while, we get a neat, coura-geous, or I wish I could do that. But most of the time, it is – insane," I replied.

We had an informative visit with Greg, who explained the area's history and how all the land around this was once useless swamp ground. He pointed out various wood lots, low spots in the multiple sections of farmland around us, and how no one would live, farm, or work in this region of Minnesota without tiling all the water into ditch systems. About an hour after parting with Greg, we rode past a farm set back 400 yards off the road with a well-kept sign reading:

Greg Schultz Tiling
Farm Drainage - GPS Mapping – Mains – Repairs
Dozer & Excavator Work

———

After sixty-two miles, we landed at Lake Allie County Park Campground, had supper, and tiredly waited for the sun to go down. The wait was well worth it as the sun setting over Lake Allie was one of the most beautiful sunsets we would see on our entire ride across America.

This is a pretty campground, and although we camped only sporadically on this journey, I was glad to have a tent along for nights like this.

Bicycle touring when you are staying at hotels and inns is referred to as "credit card touring" because you basically swipe your card each night to sleep and recharge. It has obvious advantages in terms of rest quality, access to a shower, and places to eat, and you don't need to carry as much gear for sleeping and cooking. But it is expensive, and it changes the overall experience. You meet fewer cyclists, other campers, and adventure travelers. It is less spontaneous because you need to get to a destination at the day's end versus finding a secluded spot among the trees or an isolated field to camp in whenever you feel like stopping. Our hybrid approach worked well, but next time, if there ever is a next time, we will camp more often.

———

Our last days in Minnesota were hard—really hard. The wind was a steady nine miles per hour from the southeast, which was excellent for our first ten miles or so as we pedaled with little traffic on flat roads surrounded by fields of hay. Then we turned south on US Highway 71 towards Hector, Minnesota. Highway 71 is a truck route with little to no shoulder to give room for bicycles. Traffic moved at speeds best reserved for the interstates, and situations like this call for concentration and nerve.

At its best, moving traffic is a fantastic system. There are rules, but they are fluid, offering wide variances in speed and space. The system is inhabited by large projectiles moving at tremendous speeds in opposite directions. Cars, trucks, vans, and recreational vehicles are potential fireballs hurtling, stopping, turning, and constantly adjusting themselves right and left not more than a few meters apart. The environment impacts the system, requiring drivers to adjust speed depending on the distance between vehicles based on factors like rain, air temperature, and moisture on the road, even when not raining. This entire system is at the mercy of the inhabitants of these fireballs, and the driver must intuitively make all the available adjustments every six to eight seconds with the assumption that the pilots in all the rolling missiles will behave predictably and according to the fluid rules of the system. This requires knowledge, skill, mutual trust, and a focus even with distractions.

Disruptive events like animals crossing the road, passengers, pedestrians, and cyclists can alter the operation of the organism. But the most terrifying of all for a cyclist is a driver who texts. A driver texting on his or her cell phone can drift in almost any direction, slowing down, speeding up, moving right or left, behaving in contradiction to what all the handlers of the other meteorites anticipate.

Later, we would piece it together. She had been texting.

Her small blue pickup truck narrowly missed Cheryl by swerving left. As Highway 71 is a two-lane highway, the driver quickly corrected to her right to avoid oncoming traffic. This jerk of motion, along with the wind and her right-swinging momentum, catapulted a tower of newly chromed truck wheels from the back of her pickup into the air. At this, the driver in the 18-wheeler behind her locked his brakes, stopping within inches of us.

Three chromed truck wheels pitched violently over the embankment yards ahead of me. We pulled over, as did the pickup. The tractor-trailer, smelling of burning brake pads, stopped, as did all traffic behind it. The pickup driver jumped out, we jumped off, and the tractor-trailer driver--he just sat, his face white as a ghost.

I got off my bike and went down the embankment to pick up two wheels; I estimated they weighed in at twenty pounds each and shivered a bit, thinking about what it would have been to be hit by these flying rockets. I walked them back up the hill to the pickup's driver, where she promptly started yelling at me.

"This road is too busy. You have no business being here."

I said nothing and gave her the wheel rims. To which she replied,

"What are you thinking? Can't you see this is a major highway?"

Cheryl, regaining her composure, was not in the mood to be chastised by this obviously texting driver. She firmly replied,

"Maybe tying down your load on a day this windy would be a good idea."

Although a bit proud of her for standing up for herself, I was not interested in seeing her start a fistfight with this woman, as I was sure she would lose -- even if I joined her in the skirmish. We mounted our bikes and continued on our way.

A mile down the road, Lady Google offered an option to turn west. This would put the wind at our back, and we would come into Redwood Falls from the north, crossing the river via a bridge just a mile from our hotel. We chose this variation, needing relief from buffeting winds and heavy traffic on a narrow road. The change was immediate, with wind on our left shoulder providing propulsion, not resistance, and a smooth road with little traffic. We relaxed a bit as we figured the day's excitement and challenges were over. Not so.

Seven miles later, turning south on County Road 1, we met a sign that gave me pause:

Bridge Closed Ahead
Local Traffic Only

It would take Hemingway himself to describe the anxiety and tightness of chest this sign produced. We knew that if we did not cross that bridge, we had no choice but to backtrack seven miles into a headwind to the town of Morton to the next closest bridge crossing at the Minnesota River. We'd then turn around and go seven miles back to our hotel. Adding fourteen miles to our already difficult day.

Remembering that, so far, every closed road and bridge we'd

encountered had been passable by bicycle, with every road crew so far letting us pass, we approached the bridge with hope and fear sitting together in our chests.

I could see women and men working out on the bridge—a good sign. It had a walkway that we could use to walk the bikes across—a good sign. A gentleman was working a bulldozer next to the road. He ignored me. Not such a good sign. I went up and waved him down. He hesitated—not a good sign. He shut it down and jumped out of the cab and said nothing at first— definitely not a good sign.

I explained my dilemma; he nodded, letting me know he understood—a good sign? Then hung his head a little. I knew right then we were not going over that bridge.

"I can't do it. If I let you go through and either of you got hurt, our insurance would be liable; we would be in a huge mess."

"How about I promise we won't get hurt?" I offered with a smile.

"Then you'd be God if you know what is or is not going to happen in the future." He smiled back.

"I'm not God, but as people of faith, we are willing to trust in Him to get us safely over there," I said with assurance in my voice.

With that, he turned his head slightly to his right.

"See that guy in the white pickup behind me. If I let you pass over that bridge, he'll suggest I get in my pickup, go home, and not bother coming back tomorrow. I lose my job if I let you walk over that bridge."

Recognizing defeat, I replied, "I understand, thanks, I sure don't want you or anyone to lose their job for fourteen miles," noting the total extra miles we'd need to ride in hopes of getting a lift in one of those pickups parked along the worksite.

We bid each other a nice day. Pedaling away, I saw that workman go over to the white pickup and start talking to the boss. He was pointing east - the direction we had to go. I imagined him telling the boss our predicament. I imagined the boss starting up the truck and pulling around us only to stop and drop the tailgate offering us a lift back to that bridge in Morton. I mean, we've heard, seen, and experienced Minnesota nice from so many people. It just had to happen, right?

Nope, an exception to every rule, and I guess we met the exception to Minnesota nice. Or maybe he was originally from somewhere else.

So, we turned east on a gravel road and headed toward the town of Morton seven miles away so we could cross a bridge over the river, turn around and head seven miles back west to our hotel. Fourteen extra miles at the end of an already turbulent fifty-mile day.

Not to pile on, but now is an opportune time to talk a little about gravel roads.

Like all road surfaces, one is not just like the other. Some gravel roads are hard packed, small stones, enough clay to hold down dust, and free of sand to avoid either spinning your wheels or, worse yet, bogging you down, causing you to end up taking a spill.

Vermont, for example, has over 8,000 miles of gravel roads compared to just over 5,000 miles of paved roadways. They know how to do gravel in Vermont. These roads are well maintained, hard packed, with a clay base. We love riding gravel in Vermont.

This road, marked as County 15 or Sioux Trail, had all the characteristics you DO NOT want when cycling gravel roads. Soft sand mixed with large stones, dry and dusty, it was used heavily by the large trucks hauling material from the Gordy Serbus & Sons gravel pit to and from that bridge construction site.

There is a term in the bicycling world called gravel grinding. It is a genre all its own with bicycles made specifically for gravel roads like this one. These bikes can make roads like this, which was admittedly scenic- fun. We don't have those type of bikes, and we carried over forty extra pounds of gear. It was a miserable seven miles. We ate dust, were hit by pebbles falling off big trucks, and ran out of water. Tears filled our eyes and ran down our cheeks. An hour and a half later, we made it to Morton, stopped at the local BP station for water, snacks, cool air, and a thirty-minute, air-conditioned break to revive.

Thankfully, the next seven miles back to Redwood Falls and the hotel we could almost see two hours ago were uneventful.

Now, you may wonder, do you get discouraged at these times?

Do you think about how you could bail out and be satisfied with doing 2,000 miles? Do you question your sanity at sixty-four and sixty-six years old to attempt something like a cross-country bicycle ride? Do you question all sorts of things about yourself in these times?

Yes, the answer to all those questions and more is yes. All the dark demons of self-doubt, self-loathing, and self-pity come to the surface of your mind, laughing at you with gleeful, mocking disdain.

I've previously mentioned that one of my life's axioms is to ignore the voices of negativity, which are often in our own heads. It was all we could do at this point, or else we'd give in, give up, go home. And that was not part of the plan in the spreadsheet.

———

We finally arrived at the Redwood Falls Lodge beaten and discouraged. The Lodge is a beautiful place right next to a Pizza Ranch where the Taco Texan Pizza was the highlight of our day. And as was often the case, we were both sound asleep by 8:30 PM.

Someone from Minnesota commented on our Lake Allie Instagram post, suggesting we must love the Midwest sunsets. Those necessary 8:30 PM bedtimes prevented us from seeing sunsets most of the time. We were often sound asleep by the cyclist's midnight, 9:00 PM.

Leaving Redwood Falls, we came across what I assumed was its namesake, a beautiful waterfall right on the edge of town. The interesting thing was that it was not called Redwood Falls. It is Ramsey Falls in Ramsey State Park. Go figure.

The area's history is a complex tale of the plight of the Mdewakanton Dakota Tribe of Native Americans, with all the complicated and conflicted aspects of European settlements and the treatment of Native People that mars all parts of this continent. This was not the first, and it would not be our last, reminder of the settlement, resettlement, and violence that accompanied the migration west in the mid-1800s.

We have a friend who has met difficulties in life, more than her share and certainly more than she deserves, who has often referred to the truthful cliché "This too shall pass." I thought of her as we started the day because yesterday's discouragement disappeared under the fast, smooth ride on Highway 19, also named County Road 67 and labeled Hiawatha Pioneer Trail. (This is a regular occurrence riding on roads with county numbers, state numbers, and local names. Have I mentioned my admiration of Lady Google lately? She keeps them all straight somehow.)

With the wind on our shoulder, the road wide and flat, and traffic light and polite, we found ourselves in Vesta, Minnesota, by 11:15 AM. We also found ourselves hungry. An internet search revealed a diner in Vesta that opened for breakfast and lunch and with a rating of 4.5 out of 5.0. Promising.

Vesta is a small town seemingly built up around the grain elevators which punctuate the landscape. Heading south, Highway 19 takes what felt like a random 45° turn curving west. I couldn't tell if the town was built on the curve or if it was laid down so as not to disrupt it. Six blocks long and five blocks wide, Vesta's 319 residents seem to all live only on the curve's east side.

We turned left, which was east on West North Street, rode three-and-a-half blocks, and turned right, which was south, onto North Broadway and rode two blocks south on North Broadway to the Vesta Café. A most interesting use of directional street signs.

We wondered if it was open; however, the sign said OPEN, and this looked like the type of local place we love to visit. At 11 AM, we were early for lunch and late for breakfast, and, apparently, the owner hadn't had her coffee yet. At first, she was grumpy, but after her second visit to the kitchen to get us water and then the lunch menu, she came out with spring in her step, a smile on her face, and welcoming words. I looked at Cheryl and said, "Her identical twin-- the nice sister." We chuckled.

The food was terrific and worthy of the 4.5 online score. As noon approached, locals came streaming in. We were in farm country, and young men in John Deere hats and older men in Dekalb jackets walked up to the counter, greeted the sweet twin by name, and picked up orders destined for others working in the fields. Other groups of two or four followed, found a booth or table, and sat down to eat and catch up on local *craic*. Vesta is the American heartland, with soil-stained players acting out all the parts. We were the only people in there who didn't know every other person in the place.

We had two or three folks ask about our trip, wish us well, and tell us how they hoped we would get rained out soon. Rain, or the lack of it, is the topic everywhere we go these days, and it occupied the mind, conversation, and, I am sure, the prayers of these fine people who farm in these fields and communities.

I assured them I would welcome the opportunity to ride every so often in a day or two of gentle, consistent rains. The fields, like the faces on these folks, were starting to show the stress of a summer drought.

Leaving Vesta, the day continued as differently from yesterday as could be. We made great time to Marshall, arriving before 2 PM, our earliest stop time so far.

That evening was a special treat, as Jeff and Jill and Blair and Julie drove ninety minutes, south and north respectively, to join us for supper. How do you describe gratitude for friends like this? I can only say how wealthy we are in the most magnanimous riches life offers. Our conversations were warm, sharing deep and meaningful life experiences. For them to make the effort overwhelmed us.

I'm convinced there is something inherent in people to be part of a tribe, to have connections with something that is larger than any one individual. I assume it used to be that communities sprung up of raw necessity. Protection in times of defense or shared labor for forging and farming must have been more successful when conducted as a group. I wonder now if communities grow not from the physical needs of protection and sustenance but rather from the needs of emotion and intellectual preservation. Common interests, faith, and cultural endeavors feed and protect the interior of human existence.

. . .

Friendship is a form of human connection that can be narrow and shallow or broad and deep. Perhaps both ends of this spectrum are needed. Some people you spend time with, build and reminisce with, and share a relaxation of familiarity finding reassurance. Others are needed in the dark storms of life where you need to abandon self-interests and the protection of your ego. Having friends along this spectrum makes the journey richer.

FOURTEEN

Into The Abyss

South Dakota

Approaching South Dakota, I kept thinking about old Star Trek episodes I watched as a kid. The original series, I would add. There was always some reference to force fields. Some keeping you out, some keeping you in: this is what South Dakota represented. Once we crossed that line, it was a commitment, and it was simultaneously repelling me and pulling me into the vastness of this state. Once we did travel through the force field of its border, we would have gone too far to turn around; it would keep us in, able only to go forward.

"It could be exerting a force field of some kind."

Capt. Kirk, 1966, Catpaw, *Star Trek*, Season 2, Episode 7

· · ·

But push through it we did, and the first of our thirteen days in the Mount Rushmore State were pleasant, with sunshine and light winds from the south. After leaving Brookings, most towns navigated through small farming communities of less than 200 people. Road conditions were excellent and colorful. Some roads in South Dakota are pink because they're paved with pink quartzite mined in the region. These pink ribbons of asphalt narrowing into the yellow prairie grass domed by vivid blue sky made our initial miles into South Dakota almost magical.

The scenery itself was simultaneously unremarkable and stunning. This paradox sums up our time in South Dakota. We had some of our best experiences of the ride here and yet could not wait to get out by the time we crossed into Wyoming. The changes in landscape came slowly and negligibly. We were surprised suddenly if it was different one day from what we had looked at three days earlier.

———

Eating on a cycle tour can be a challenge. We elected to limit cooking and found ourselves too frequently in America's fast-food joints, especially the omnipresent gas station convenience stores. In the east, it was Valero; Casey's in the Midwest; and by the time we hit the Mount Rushmore State, Conoco seemed to be the predominant purveyor of Lays chips, Planters peanuts, rolling hot dogs in a glass case, and diesel. Subway sandwich shops and Dollar General were the other frequented establishments that enjoyed a measurable portion of our budget.

We ate at Applebee's in Brookings one evening and needed to sit at the bar due to limited seating, once again attributed to Covid staff shortages. I remember this as the first time these pandemic-induced shortages impacted our ability to find seating at suppertime.

I sensed the couple on our left noticed our accents and asked where we were traveling from. When I mentioned New England, they shook their heads affirmatively in unison as if they thought so. They were from Pierre, which they kindly explained should be pronounced *peer*, and looked on in amazement when we said we were bicycling. I think they were more astounded that we planned to cycle through West Dakota than they were that we'd come from Boston.

Pierre, South Dakota's capital, is on the eastern shore of the Missouri River. With just under 15,000 residents, it is the nation's second-least-populated state capital. Smack in the middle of the state, Pierre is a haven for fishing and hunting and the gateway to West Dakota.

We learned South Dakotans speak of west Dakota and east Dakota almost as separate states. Virtually cut in half north to south by the Missouri River, east Dakota was not unlike the west side of Minnesota, with towns and villages frequent along any roadway.

Sitting at Applebee's that evening, we had no clue how vast, sparsely populated, and remote West Dakota would feel. Our friend from Pierre looked at us and said, "Do you know how desolate it is out there west of the Missouri?"

I mentioned that we had traveled by camper through the northern sections of the state on Route 12 a few years earlier and knew it was sparse. He just shook his head and said, "Yeah, but you're on a bicycle. There is nothing out there." Then he added a question we'd already been asked before since crossing the Mississippi:

"Are you going through the reservation?"

I said we planned to cross the Missouri at Fort Thompson, about sixty miles downstream from Pierre, and I saw on the map that we would cross into a recreational area but didn't know about a reservation. He mentioned we would go through the Crow Creek Sioux Reservation.

"Be real careful," he said with genuine concern in his voice.

I wondered what we would encounter. I also remember similar statements we had received when planning travels in Mexico and Peru years ago. There, we met good people living their lives and showing kindness to strangers. I expected the same in Fort Thompson.

By now, our ride across a continent had poignantly validated a lesson learned across life. People everywhere are wonderfully welcoming, curious, and well-wishing. But a fear exists in humanity that posits a contrary idea. People we know and understand are inherently good; people we don't know much about or don't understand are inherently to be feared.

Riding in the eastern states, when asked where we were going, we explained our plans and would often get the question, "You're not going through the western states are you?" They would go on to explain that people there have guns and will shoot us for no apparent reason.

Riding in Indiana and parts of rural Illinois, we would hear the question phrased differently: "You're not going through Chicago are you? Especially the south side, that is really dangerous."

Pedaling through Minnesota and eastern South Dakota, we would emphatically and simultaneously be questioned and warned, "You not going through the reservation are you? You can't do that; it's really not safe."

We would ride through every place of these fears and warnings and only experience the warmth and encouragement of people who called those places home.

In 2021, America was filled with a controversial pandemic, contested election counts, conspiracy, mistrust, and overall general acrimony. I pondered why we humans are so prone to viewing people differently from ourselves with anger and suspicion, sometimes outright hatred. We had observed this tension across the nation in signs, slogans, and conversations; some we had heard directly; others we overheard. Yet, when we connected with people one-on-one, it was never maliciousness and mistrust we encountered -- it was always curiosity and good wishes.

Within a couple of weeks, we would cycle on a thinly traveled road and pass a sign in a remote corner of a vast area of rural beauty with no buildings within sight that read:

Keep Out
I have a gun
And a bulldozer

What enemies, what threat, what experiences could prompt such fear that someone would come and take away whatever this soul was terrified of losing? That sign seemed to exemplify a constant undercurrent that was almost paranormal. The presence of something sinister but, frankly, was not real.

It seems we humans can think of others as subhuman when we can label them with something we fear or don't understand. By that label, other people become a concept, idea, or non-living entity, which makes it easy to see them as the source of our fears, or perceived fears. We no longer see a person with empathy and assumed to be living their life as best they can, pursuing happiness and self-respect just like us. We see some things to avoid or change, or worst of all to be eliminated somehow.

Years ago, I participated in a discussion on the seminal book on surviving the Holocaust, *Man's Search for Meaning* by Viktor Frankl. One of the speakers, Harold, was the grandson of an Auschwitz survivor. Harold spoke of Frankl's experiences in the book with passionate emotion, choking up with tears as he recalled similar accounts his grandfather shared with him about his time in the same death camp.

One of the listeners, we'll call her Esther, joined in conversation about the book, asking deep, important, and personal questions. She demonstrated immense empathy and compassion for his feelings, and her participation in his discourse was considerate, making Harold more impressive and successful than he would have been without her participation.

Esther had grown up in rural Iran, or Persia as she insisted, and intuitively, I approached her later in the day and thanked her for her encouraging contribution to the discussion. But something prompted me to ask, "So, did you read the book?"

"I wouldn't read that Zionist propaganda if you held a gun to my head," she said quickly, and in that moment I didn't know what to say.

Then, a little softer, she added, "Would you ever include a book about some other holocaust in this program?"

"Such as the Armenian genocide of World War I?" I asked.

I watched her face soften at my answer. I had gained her respect and trust because of my willingness to try and understand. Plus, she was surprised that I even knew about the Armenian genocide.

Over the next half year, I witnessed Esther and Harold become genuine friends. They encouraged each other professionally and improved each other during warm and friendly conversations in class. They cared about each other and shared openly life's successes and challenges.

I learned numerous lessons observing this relationship. The willingness at the personal level to be vulnerable, transparent, and reassuring to an individual who, in anonymity, would be lumped in the labeled group you are obligated to detest was simultaneously inspirational and baffling—a tangible sample of cognitive dissonance.

———

Leaving Brookings, we headed west on State Road 14, expecting we'd spend the night in De Smet, about forty-five miles away. As the day progressed, so did the force of the direct west wind. Rolling into Lake Preston, we battled headwinds and were knocked around by the slipstreams from tractor-trailers. The wind was enough to make us find something, if anything, available for lodging.

The Lake Preston Motel and Bait Shop was the only establishment in town, and after stopping at the bait shop, which served as the motel's check-in desk, we shortened our day and took a roomette, a two-room space with a bedroom, bath, and kitchen.

The motel is out of the 1950s, well, maybe 1940s: one story, flat roof, a single chair positioned like a sentry at each door. The parking lot was a crumbling surface of old asphalt, potholes, and gravel bordered by cement tire stops positioned in front of each room. Our room had two beds and two chairs set on either side of a steel-legged table. The dimly lit kitchen alcove had a small stove, sink, and coffee maker. Everything was the most modern of furnishings--when FDR was the President.

It was also the first and only time Cheryl pulled out her sleeping bag and slept in it on top of the bed, as she was unwilling to climb into the lumpy bed regardless of how much I assured her the sheets were clean.

It was Sunday, and the only option for supper was gas station gourmet yet again. We sat outside in the evening, eating our chips and salsa while swapping travel stories with four motorcyclists traveling home to Minnesota from Yellowstone National Park. They assured me of the wisdom in circumventing Yellowstone. After waiting ninety minutes to check through the gate, the group entered the park from West Yellowstone, Montana, the lowest traffic entrance. They turned around and left after only going five miles because traffic was bumper to bumper and crawling with RVs and cars stopping at every instance of a wildlife sighting.

This account of Yellowstone gave me confidence in our plan: we were to cut north before reaching Cody, Wyoming, to Livingston, Montana, then ride over the pass to Bozeman before cutting back southwest, swinging through Virginia City, Twin Bridges, Sula, and Hamilton to reach Missoula. But I remained plagued with self-doubt and trepidation at the idea of carving a route that took us off the highways routinely traveled by other cyclists. This feeling of ambiguity would be a companion for weeks to come.

With Midwest (that is to say weak) coffee for breakfast and nothing at Boomer's Convenience Store to tempt us, we left early, hoping that De Smet would offer a local breakfast joint. The Oxbow proved to be all we'd been looking for and made up for our lack of good eats the day before. The owner, who also served as cook, waiter, and cashier, was efficient, friendly, and another example of hardworking prairie people who do what is needed to make it all work.

De Smet is also the center of Laura Ingalls Wilder country. We'd seen signs letting us know we were on the Laura Ingalls Wilder Historic Highway since joining RT 14 southwest of Marshall. De Smet is Laura's homestead, and the local cemetery is the resting place for many of her relatives. There are tours for adults and children, and the town's promoters employ many ways to keep the memory of her Little House on the Prairie alive.

———

Because of the disruption of our unexpected stop in Lake Preston, Huron was our stop that day. And, were it not for that unexpected slowdown, I would have missed one of the most inspiring encounters we ever had while cycle touring.

I met Tamara in Huron, South Dakota. A little later than our typical start time, I wheeled my bike out of our hotel and down the hallway, and she, smiling broadly, asked, "Where are you going?"

"Well, today my wife and I are heading to Wessington Springs, but we hope to go as far as the Pacific Ocean," I answered a little hesitantly because I didn't want to sound like I was bragging.

"Wow, that's exciting, where did you start?" she asked, still smiling.

"Well, we started in Boston, Massachusetts, so it's a been a long ride so far." Now, I was really trying to minimize it because I for sure didn't want to sound arrogant. When meeting young people, I didn't mind saying we'd come from the East Coast, but I felt self-conscious when telling someone around our age what we were doing.

"That's amazing. Have you enjoyed it?"

"We've had a wonderful time. Some difficult days, but overall, it has been the fulfillment of a dream. How about yourself? What brings you to Huron today?"

Then, without losing her warm smile, Tamara explained she was here with her family to attend the memorial and burial service for her husband that afternoon at 1:30 PM. She told me that he had passed away from cancer a week ago.

"I'm so sorry; you have my sympathy. Was it expected? Had he fought with it a long time?" I asked

"No, not at all. He died as a result of a mix-up of chemo drugs at the treatment center. It was a mistake, and it took his life needlessly. It wasn't supposed to be terminal."

At this point, I admit I felt stupid for spending time waxing on about my bicycle trip, which felt rather hollow then. I said something to the effect that she seemed to be handling this well and didn't seem angry or bitter at what happened.

"Oh, I am not upset; he is with the Lord, and I'm old enough to know it won't be long until we're together again. Would you like to meet my family?" she asked.

Without waiting for me to answer, Tamara walked a short way down the hall and knocked on a door. She introduced me to her two beautiful and dressed-for-the-service granddaughters. She explained my trip, where I had come from, and how exciting it must be to bicycle that far.

The two girls smiled politely, although with a bemused look on their faces, and wished me a good trip. I had the feeling they were used to their grandmother making connections with strangers.

I assured Tamara I would pray for her and her family, and I rolled my bike out the door. I pondered that meeting throughout the day and many times since. Tamara would've been married fifty-four years on July 1st. She had to be one of the most magnanimous people I have ever met. Her faith, strength, lack of resentment, and genuine interest in me were inspiring. Tamara was also the epitome of "no whinging." Not one syllable of complaint or self-pity.

It is a great gift to exercise the power of and redirection of emotions the way she demonstrated, and I thought of the proverb "He that is slow to anger is better than the mighty; and he that ruleth his spirit than he that taketh a city."

Walking out the hotel's door, I realized that were it not for the events of two days earlier, events I complained about, I would not have met Tamara, and my trip would have been diminished because of it. It was also a cue that reminded me that I am not the center of the universe.

————

Midway between Huron and the Missouri River sits the town of Wessington Springs. We may long forget the best known towns and villages of our journey, but we will long remember Wessington Springs as the embodiment of what cycle touring gives you that traveling by car or plane does not.

Located on the north side of Route 34, we climbed the newly paved road up a short but relatively steep hill, turned right, and entered Wessington Springs with yet another Dollar General on the east side of Dakota Avenue and the Hardware Hank store on the west.

It was almost a habit to stop at a Dollar General by this point in the trip. Doris welcomed us to town while ringing up our Gatorade and asked where we were going. When she heard we were planning to camp in the town park for the night, she picked up her cell and called a local friend who runs a B&B on the north side of town to see if she had room for us.

She was booked, which turned out to be providential for us. Camping the next two nights in the center of this oasis on the prairie became a delightful treat. In short order, the town populace seemed to know we were there, and people were helpful and interested in our journey.

In addition to Doris, local waitresses, and families who used the park in the early evenings, we met Harold, who would exercise his dog twice daily. Harold was polite, soft-spoken, and reserved. That is, until he talked to the dog. He would break out into name-calling and adjectives with a lexicon that would make a tipsy sailor blush. Harold talked with us each time he drove through, sharing how he'd farmed in the area all his life, traveled around Europe for three months with his daughter years ago, and now in his mid-eighties, was caring for his wife, who had Alzheimer's.

Harold spoke of the difficulties in distributing a large family farm. His son wasn't interested in continuing the farming life, and his recent meetings with attorneys to set up what to do with his life's work when he passed on were frustrating for him. He explained that the town's residents were planning to renovate the nearby pool in the fall and that it was leaking, and how much it meant to this small town. His kindness and transient friendship made our almost-three-day stay here personal.

America's Midwest has abundant villages like this, with town parks open to campers. Some, like Wessington Springs, come with electricity, a crushed stone pad, a picnic table, and water. All for $15 per night on the honor system.

We also met an eastbound cyclist named Scott. We were sitting at the picnic table on our first afternoon, and he saw us, turned onto the gravel road, and rolled up. Scott sat down, and we visited for an hour or so, sharing experiences, fears, hard days, and best times. It turned out Scott was traveling the same route we planned through Wyoming and South Dakota, so his information on what would be coming up for us was helpful. He had begun his ride in West Yellowstone, Montana, and told us about riding through Yellowstone National Park. The report about traffic and wildlife was ambivalent, which left me unsure of our plans to cut north and skip Yellowstone. Cheryl, however, was resolute in her decision not to cycle in Yellowstone, so my uncertainty was immaterial.

The Wessington Springs City Park has mown grass with shade trees and is adjacent to the town's baseball field and a large community swimming pool, complete with a high dive. The pool is available for $3 daily, including access to locker rooms and showers. In the 103° degree heat, it was a welcome respite.

Swimming in the pool, I was transported back to Manchester, Connecticut's Verplank pool where my cousins and I learned to swim and spent many summer days jumping from a high dive just like this one. I spent an hour or so texting pictures of this place to my cousins Carol, Cathy, Peg, and Janet, reminiscing about those years and the times we had.

I spent hours during our stay here thinking about what it was like growing up in a community like Wessington Springs. Schools were out for the summer, and moms spent afternoons with young kids in and out of the pool. Lifeguards would pace back and forth and whistle at boys giving too much aggravating attention to their latest crush. Just like Verplank, this pool took a break at 2:30 PM, requiring everyone under eighteen to get out of the water so older folks had time alone swimming, and I suspect the lifeguards needed a break, too.

Around 5 PM, dads coming from work joined their families for a swim and a cookout, just like my father did on those summer evenings years ago after work at Aetna Life & Casualty in Hartford. A couple of hours later, cars, pickups, and walkers started streaming into the park for a baseball game. It was complete with an announcer, local advertisements, and cheering from the couple of hundred spectators who were as into the action as any major league crowd ten times the size.

It was all very 1960s in its impression on me. I had a melancholy sense of seeing my childhood as if I was at a drive-in movie and my boyhood was playing on the big screen. That afternoon and evening were the only times I was homesick during the entire trip, wishing I could ride around the corner and be home.

It was on our second night that the thunderstorm raucously blew through. We had watched the colorful sunset and heard thunder off to the west, but by dark, it had quieted down, and we slithered (the only word to describe it adequately) into our tiny Tarptent. As we drifted asleep, a magnificent CLAP brought us to full consciousness. In what seemed like seconds, the rain pelted our tent, and winds whipped so hard I imagined this was the sound of a machine gun in war.

At first we were frightened, thinking about lightning strikes, trees crashing down on us, and the possibility of such wind ripping the Tarptent apart. But then we just started laughing, both of us. There was absolutely nothing to do but wait it out. We could have run, but where? Under the trees? Not a good option. The pool house or locker rooms? Locked. The baseball dugout would be the best option, but it was at least a quarter of a mile across the open field. So, we just laughed.

Twenty violent minutes, and then, nothing. It all stopped as fast as it began. The Tarptent didn't tear, didn't even leak; the lightning didn't hit us; all the trees and branches were still grounded and attached. Did we drift back to sleep? Nope. Now filled with adrenaline pumping through the systems, we were awake.

So, we talked. About life, family, friends close, friends lost, and friends who had moved on. We ruminated on what life would be like after this trip and what we wanted to look forward to, given we expected more freedom of choice and time. We spoke of letting go of ambition and what, if anything, had our efforts in life accomplished. It was a good visit and remedy for the melancholy musings of the previous hours.

Soon after the storm ended, the local town constable came driving through and shined his spotlight on our site. Given we were obviously there with the tent and bikes still standing, he moved on. It was clear he knew we were camping in town; he came through to make sure we were all right. I thought about Bill, the cyclist we met outside Cleveland who told us that South Dakota will change your life. People like Tamara, Doris, Harold, and an overnight town constable made that very true. This would be reinforced again the next day on our visit to the reservation.

———

It was immediately evident that the morning was cooler and a bit overcast. We broke camp, waved at Scott peddling out of town, had a final visit from Harold, grabbed gas station fare for breakfast (of course), and started towards the Missouri River. We spent a restful night at the Lode Star Hotel in Fort Thompson, yards from the Lode Star Casino on the Crow Creek Reservation.

The following morning at the reservation convenience store, we purchased breakfast, a few snacks, and the day's quota of Gatorade. Walking out the door, we met Larry Covered Stone. Larry, wearing dirt-stained jeans and a sleeveless grey T-shirt with an American Flag with American Classic blazing across its chest, asked about our ride. He was interested and encouraging when we told him we started on the East Coast. When he asked what the best part of our ride had been, I told him it was meeting encouraging and interested people like him. He laughed and began to tell us about his life.

When I mentioned we were heading west and expected to go through Kennebec today, about thirty miles on, Larry told us about the last time he was in Kennebec. He was playing little league baseball and described the trip and games as if it were a month ago, not decades. Larry looked to be about fifty, and it struck me how his little league trip had as much memory to him as our trip across the country would have to us.

Larry told us about the Missouri as well, its fishing heritage, and about the time as a young boy that he tried to swim across the river and almost drowned.

"At the time, I thought it was about half a mile. Turned out it was more. A lot more," he chuckled, but I sensed the memories of fear and terror were fresh.

Bidding us goodbye, Larry looked at us and said, "Keep the kind spirit, and you'll meet nice people everywhere you go." How true.

As I have pondered Larry's axiom since, I realized he was giving us counsel for life, as much as it is for a bicycle tour across a continent. I've also wondered if angels, unaware, sometimes wear dirty jeans and sleeveless grey T-shirts blaring an American Flag across their chest.

A short time later, as we crossed the Missouri, I thought about a young Larry trying to swim from east to west Dakota across this expanse of water and how years later, that still viscerally impacted him.

———

We were now geographically halfway through South Dakota. Years ago, a co-worker of mine thru-hiked the Appalachian Trail from Georgia to Maine. Being familiar with the beauty of Virginia, I imagined she must have loved walking the spine of the Shenandoah Mountains. Instead, she talked about it like someone speaks about a long tedious project.

"Ugh, long, long, and more long," is how she described it.

I was startled and replied, "Yeah, but it's beautiful, isn't it?"

"Noooo! It's too hot by the time you hit Skyline Drive, plus it's crowded at the top. More hikers give up and cave in Virginia than any other state. It's a curse, really. You cross the state line with euphoria, but soon the towns become such a temptation you are ready to throw everything you worked for away for a day off, which turns into a week that becomes a bus ride home. You thought you were leaving a job and the day-to-day grind, but the routine and monotony have replaced the excitement and novelty. I almost quit in Virginia."

Thinking about that talk now brought back memories of people I'd known who had a great start in a career, a marriage, or a relocation with all the excitement those new experiences offer. Often, at the beginning of something, we are energized, committed, charged with innovation, and thrilled at the prospects. Then we hit Virginia, or west Dakota, our midlife in an AT thru-hike or cross-country cycle tour. And, like life itself, what once was new is now patently familiar; what was once an effort and challenge is routine and easy; what was once a goal is now something we think we missed or is too far over the horizon.

At this point, like my friend in Virginia, we might be tempted to give up. She didn't, and post-Virginia she hit new highlights walking through states on her way to a summit completion. Life is like this, a temptation to bail on something just before we crest a rise that would make all the difference between regret and realization. A wise man once gave me an equation that went:

$$P-P+P=P$$

Perspiration minus Panic plus Perseverance equals Prosperity

Mid-life, mid-hike, or mid-ride is a danger zone. Those who press on and look at the well-known with fresh eyes are the ones who see the view from Katahdin, wheel tires into the Pacific Ocean, or reap the benefits of wisdom that only years of labor affords.

I pondered if South Dakota would be our Virginia, the midlife point of a ride that had held my imagination for years. Would I be the cyclist who bailed to an airport home, or would it be the state of perseverance where we pressed through the doldrums with its temptations of cynicism or the allure that caused us to go to someplace else, thinking it to be more adventurous, free, or glamorous?

Our first full day in west Dakota didn't do a thing to dispel the idea. At one point on top of a rise, I looked out in all directions and saw – nothing. No trees, buildings, telephone or electric lines, or cars. Just one long ribbon of asphalt stretching to a dot on the horizon.

The thing is – it thrilled me.

Cheryl was in a different place; hating the isolation and barren landscape of west Dakota made her homesick. But with the endurance her Swiss heritage imparted, she just pressed on without complaining.

So, no, South Dakota would not be our Virginia, and like midlife, we would pass through it – tested, not disrupted or destroyed, bruised a bit, but convinced the Pacific was reachable.

———

The final half of South Dakota became a blur of happenings. A restless sleep in Kadoka due to bedbugs; an afternoon in Wall, home to the famous Wall Drug filled to the brim with Americana kitsch; a serendipitous rendezvous with friends Wes and Esther at the Dairy Queen on their return from Livingston, Montana; and being followed off I-90 by a South Dakota State Trooper who was checking on us to make sure we knew what we were doing.

We met Michelle on a middle-of-nowhere road in rural west Dakota. She pulled over and literally screamed with delight at finding people. She had been lost and needed directions back to the highway, which we were able to help her with. We talked with Michelle long enough to share why she was driving to Seattle from New Jersey, her profession as an acupuncturist, a bit about her family, and how excited she was to start a new chapter in life.

On reaching Rapid City, I had a moment of déjà vu pedaling along the unassuming Rapid Creek. The last time I was here was the Summer of 1972, just weeks after this small stream had devastated the city.

Fifteen inches of rain had fallen in less than six hours in the Black Hills about twenty miles west of town, and the cascading wall of water swept through Rapid City, destroying over 1,300 homes and 5,000 cars and killing over 230 people. Today, there is a rebuilt city, a creek-side park, a bike path, and signage marking points of interest from those terrible hours. I had pieces like a memory collage from that 1972 car ride: mud-strewn sidewalks, broken-out storefronts, and cars still piled on top of one another.

Rapid City and the Black Hills are gateways to some of America's icons. The Mount Rushmore and Crazy Horse Monuments, Custer State and Black Hills National Forest, and the Motorcycle mecca of Sturgis are all a short distance away. For the iconic American Road Trip, this is the beginning of the West with its Rocky Mountains, big rivers, and majestic peaks.

Our last hours in South Dakota were fitting for the ending of an allegorical ride through midlife. We found ourselves riding from the prairie grass-blanketed plains into green foothills, leaving Sturgis towards the burg of Belle Fourche just to the east of the Wyoming border. We left South Dakota with ambivalence. It was beautiful and the people were some of the friendliest. But it is long, filled with extremes, and has a sense of loneliness attached to it.

We saw homes that would fit in America's wealthiest neighborhoods and others that reminded me of the poor mountain villages we passed hiking in the Peruvian Andes. We were elated at times and on the verge of tears at others. Seeing friends in Wall was so lovely and encouraging. The next night in Kadoka, bed bugs had me itching for two days.

I loved the sparse landscape along the Missouri River and felt sad at the plight of Native Americans. I was giddy at seeing how far we'd come when looking at Google Maps then intimidated remembering we were getting closer to crossing of the Big Horn Mountains outside of Buffalo, Wyoming.

I was confident about the choices made when scouting our route, but I was anxious and indecisive, wondering if it would be better to go through Yellowstone rather than circle north through more remote areas into Bozeman.

And so, after twelve cycling days, one rest day, one violent thunderstorm, over 450 miles pedaled, and countless wonderful people encountered, we crossed into Wyoming on Rt 24, seven miles east of Aladdin, Wyoming.

FIFTEEN

Out of the Malaise, Into Adulthood

Wyoming

The hamlet of Aladdin, Wyoming, rests at an elevation of 3,790 feet, with a population of fifteen, one hotel, one restaurant, a general store, and one post office. All are co-located within a hundred feet of each other. The Aladdin Motel was a neat place with a great little cabin. We met Mr. Rogers, a rancher who, along with his two employees, owned everything except the post office. Aladdin also connected us back on the ACA Parks, Peaks, and Prairie route we'd left just after Wall, South Dakota. Impressive for this little hamlet.

A 7 AM breakfast followed an excellent night's sleep for an early start to Devil's Tower.

Although this cycle tour was about something other than visiting tourist sites, Devil's Tower was one place I wanted to see. I don't know why; perhaps it was the idea that scientists still are not certain how this column of columns came about. I felt an affinity to that ambiguity. So much of life had seemed to erode now that I was retired: less responsibilities, no rhythm of a paycheck, no association of a tribe or career objectives. I pondered whether this stark tower with everything around it eroded, a metaphor for the last third of my life in so-called retirement.

The 1828 version of *Webster's Dictionary of the English Language* defines retirement as four things:

RETI'REMENT, *noun*

1. The act of withdrawing from a company or from public notice or station.
2. The state of being withdrawn; as the *retirement* of the mind from the senses.
3. Private abode; habitation secluded from much society or from public life.
4. Private way of life.

The idea we now associate with retirement is both new and outdated at the same time. Society's current assertions of retirement are defined by patterns and expectations laid down in the 1950s. Before this, people continued to add value, stay productive, and remain included in work and community until they died or couldn't participate any longer in any capacity. Withdrawal and seclusion because you've reached a certain age were not part of the mental model.

The current version of Mr. Webster's online lexicon is even more distressing:

RETI'REMENT, *noun, adjective*

1. A retiring or being retired; specif., withdrawal from work, business, etc. because of age. Noun
2. The act of retiring or the state of being retired.
3. *The retirement of debt.* Noun

4. Of, having to do with, or for retirement or retired persons.
5. *A retirement community.* Adjective
6. The voluntary termination of employment upon reaching a certain age. Verb See <u>retire</u>.

If you follow the link for retire, you'll read:

1. To go to bed. Verb
2. To go away, retreat, or withdraw to a private, sheltered, or secluded place. Verb
3. To withdraw from one's occupation or position, especially upon reaching a certain age; stop working. Verb
4. To give up one's work, business, career, etc., esp. because of advanced age. Verb
5. To move away or withdraw, as for rest or seclusion. Verb

Appealing, don't you think?

Cresting a hill in mid-afternoon, Devil's Tower appeared on the horizon. I stopped and asked Lady Google how far away we were. Fifteen miles off in the distance, and it still had a presence. That, to me, was a better symbol. I wanted to be like that: straight, standing unrelenting against the erosion of time.

We cycled thirty-five miles and over 2,100 feet of elevation gain from Aladdin to Devil's Tower. The day was our biggest elevation gain since the Berkshires of Massachusetts, and we arrived early at the Devils Tower KOA, scoring the last cabin they had - with AC. It was brutally hot with temps reaching 100°, and although the pool was crowded, it was wet and cool.

———

We decided to begin our ride the next day at 5 AM to try and beat the expected heat and afternoon wind. Sixty miles to the small city of Gillette had us both a little concerned. Before going to sleep, we also smelled and saw smoke from wildfires burning in the Sundance, Wyoming, area, about twenty-five miles to the southeast of us. It made us a bit uneasy, but little did we know that smell, apprehension, and the hazy sky would now be our companion and nemesis.

———

It was Independence Day, and the Tower was almost red in the early morning light. Another effect of smoke in the air was the diffusing of sunrise and sunset light into brilliant reds, purples, oranges, and blues across the sky and mountains. We had views of the Tower on our right and vast ranch lands on the left as we climbed Route 24, heading towards Moorcroft and another intersection with I-90, where we would parallel the ribbon of asphalt again for thirty miles into Gillette.

Leaving Moorcroft we had picked up US Route 16, an old road that today runs from Rapid City, South Dakota, to the eastern entrance of Yellowstone National Park. Initially, RT 16 began in Detroit, and like many of these roads, it was the early underpinning for the pavement that would become the Interstate Highway System. Route 16 shares topography with I-90 and is now referred to as the Mount Rushmore Road. By the time it terminates at the entrance to Yellowstone, it runs concurrently with US Routes 14 and 20; another reminder of how our cycling passage follows the history of America's western migration from Indian Wars, railroads, presidential monuments, and National Parks.

Riding 16 into Gillette, we learned this boom-to-bust city of over 30,000 bills itself as the Energy Capital of the Nation, being centrally located in an area of coal, oil, and methane gas production. The city was founded in the early 1890s as a significant stop on the Chicago, Burlington, and Quincy Railroad and continues to greet visitors arriving on the I-90 corridor with thousands of orange, red, and green railroad cars and locomotives, graffiti-covered and standing idle waiting to be called into service.

Route 16 would also be our road for a section of cycling that had filled our minds with anxiety since the early planning days:

Gillette to Buffalo and Buffalo to Ten Sleep. These would be the most remote miles and the highest elevation gain, respectively, and they would be back-to-back days of long miles, and 6,400 feet of elevation gain to reach and then cross the Big Horn Mountains at Powder River Pass, the highest point in our ride at 9,666 feet. From the pass, we would drop the steepest elevation loss. A drop of 5,308 feet over twenty-eight miles into Ten Sleep Canyon. All of this within the next 158 miles. I had worried for months about our capability to do the miles between services, the climb up to Powder River, and the steep descent safely into Ten Sleep.

We left Gillette before 7 AM with the knowledge that we had one stop at thirty-eight miles in Spotted Horse and a second at seventy miles in Clearmont. We also knew there was nothing between Gillette and Spotted Horse and nothing from Spotted Horse to Clearmont. We had to either camp a night at Spotted Horse and go to Buffalo the next day or go the seventy miles to Clearmont and camp there. We never considered going the full hundred miles in one day.

Our morning ride was smooth and windless, and although we were climbing, it felt flat. We left the Fairfield Inn & Suites, riding past those ever-present icons of American progress, Hiltons, La Quinta, Ramadas, and Holiday Inns all packed into a square mile. Why do we do that in this country? Drug stores, car dealerships, and hotel chains are bunched together like penguins on an iceberg. It makes every small city indistinguishable from the next. And of course, Starbucks, which provided us with breakfast that day, like it had and would frequently.

The American West is different than the east. In the east, one town mutates into the next without the intermission of vast landscapes. But here, within an hour of our gingerbread latte, hazelnut misto, and croissants, we were cycling a narrow road through landscape that would have passed for the Serengeti. Well, had it not been for the telephone poles and wire fencing.

We saw Spotted Horse about a mile away after a gentle rise and left-hand turn in the road. In the vast emptiness of the Wyoming prairie, we first saw four or five trees standing on the vista. Spotted

Horse is marked only by those trees shading a small white and red-trimmed building twenty-five feet off the road and marked with a red, white, and blue old Standard Gas station sign. It reminded me of Route 66 roadside museums seen in places like Odell and Pontiac, Illinois, not the Serengeti.

This iconic 1940s structure serves as a tavern, restaurant, and offered a campground around the back. It no longer pumps gas, and the restaurant and bar is noticeably often visited, and noticeably rarely cleaned. However, the burger and fries were excellent fuel for our afternoon. Since we had moved far faster than expected, we finished lunch before noon and were heading to Clearmont ahead of schedule, assuming we would camp there for the night and have a short thirty miles the next day into Buffalo.

We reached Clearmont before 5 PM. This village is a microcosm of many towns in the vast open range of large western states. Route 16 split the town literally in half. On our left to the east one block was Devon Street, and to our right one block lay West Street. Both ran parallel to Route 16, and each was bisected perpendicularly by five side streets.

At the southern end of town, we stopped at the Clear Creek Stop, a combination gas station, restaurant, and campground common in these little towns. After getting some food, including a welcome ice cream, we rested for a few minutes at a picnic table, graciously set up in the shade. It was here we first talked about going on or spending the night at the campground.

With over three hours of daylight left, Lady Google told us the ride to Buffalo was virtually flat, and the wind was at our back. So, we were game to attempt our trip's only one-hundred-mile day of cycling, obviously forgetting our promise back in Auburn, Indiana, never to ride a ninety-mile day again. As we left town, we passed a running sprinkler that was wetting the roadside shoulder as well as the lawn.

"Wait!" Cheryl called out to me as I circumvented the spray. I stopped and looked back at her, puzzled.

"Ride through it. I want a picture," she said.

"Huh?"

"It'll make a great picture," she insisted

"Sure," I said spinning around and riding through the spray.

"Again. It didn't come out that good. Ride through it again," she persisted.

So, I obediently turned around and rode through that shower of glistening droplets a second time. It was not hard to do on a hot, dry, and sun-drenched late afternoon in small-town Wyoming. The thing is, as I write this now, I don't remember if she rode through that sprinkler herself or not. Was that a good picture or just a way to tell me to go soak my head after making the case for riding a hundred-mile day?

There are times and events in life that work out differently from the angst and fears we imagine. A year ago, a hundred-mile cycling day, or century ride as it is called, in remote Wyoming would have elicited an uneasy laugh or scornful "no way." Today, it simply seemed like the reasonable thing to do—no big deal. It was a lesson not to erect self-imposed limits or barriers that become achievable with time, experience, and a more open mind.

But this wasn't the only lesson the day imparted. As we rode into the parking lot of the Hampton Inn & Suites, Buffalo, my Strava odometer read 99.4 miles as I pulled up to the door. I laughed out loud. Turning to Cheryl I said, "Two laps around this parking lot and we will have a one-hundred-mile day. Our first century together."

"I don't need that. Go for it if you want to," she replied.

This is typical for her. There is no need to earn bragging rights or have something in her story that she can tell people about. Cheryl was matter-of-fact about this, as she was about so many things throughout the ride—throughout life. She did not need accolades and validation from other people to carry a sense of self-worth.

This is one of the many things I admire about her. It is not one of the traits I carry. I am prone to needing confirmation from others. Another artist to give credibility to my creations. A person of higher rank, more education, or bigger status had to acknowledge what I did if I was to be convinced within myself I wasn't really the imposter the voice in my head said I was. I often looked for that in restrained ways. Was it ego? Pride? Insecurity?

What was the point of riding in a circle for six-tenths of a mile to say I rode that distance? What is it that we measure ourselves by? Did that .6 of distance make me better? Is the day better? If I said to someone, "We rode a one-hundred-mile day," would it be true since it was close enough? Had I ridden two or three circles around that hotel parking lot, I could say, backed up with data, that I rode a century on this journey. A measurable milestone that would add some badge proving my accomplishment to the ride.

In the seconds that followed, with all those questions rolling around in my head, I lifted my tired leg up and over the seat, hit the FINISH button on Strava showing 99.6, and walked into the lobby – smiling.

I thought a lot about this and the questions of ego, insecurity, and the need we humans have for external validation over the miles in the days and weeks that followed. In summary, I think letting go of ambition is a companion to letting go of ego.

––––––––––

Being a day early into Buffalo permitted us to take a zero day. Well, a "nero," actually, since we did ride into town for errands, including shipping some stuff forward to save weight. As I outlined earlier, the next two days would be spent riding over the highest pass, steepest grade, and longest downhill of the trip, and all within the next sixty-three miles. We rested, swam, ate well, and had one of the more interesting exchanges with people, reminding us of how small and random the world is.

When checking into the Hampton, a family lined up behind us and asked a few questions about our ride. The following day at breakfast, Sara approached and tentatively asked, "Are you the couple who checked in last night and are riding across the country?"

Smiling to be friendly, but also because I assumed she wasn't exactly sure we were the right people now that we were showered, most likely smelled better, and didn't have florescent yellow jackets on, I answered, "We are."

"That's amazing. I would so like to do that someday," she went on.

"I hope you get to; it has been a wonderful experience. Are you from around here?" I asked.

"No, we took our boys on vacation to Missoula, Montana, and are heading home to Indiana."

As her husband, Andy, walked up next to her, I asked, "Oh, where in Indiana are you from?"

"Indianapolis. We own a coffee roaster there and had combined our vacation in Missoula to visiting some other roasters to share experiences and get ideas," Andy explained, joining the conversation.

"Very nice. I love coffee, and Missoula is on our route. We hope to be there in about three weeks. We went through Indiana, of course. No offense, but the roads were some of the worst we've encountered so far. Cheryl is still talking about writing Secretary Buttigieg to encourage him to spend some of that federal infrastructure money on his home state."

They didn't react to my attempt at some humor, so I went on to change the subject.

"We rode north of Indy, through Valparaiso."

"Oh, I grew up in a little town just outside of Valpo," Sara piped up.

"Really? We have friends we met for dinner in Valpo who live in a little town called LaCrosse. Do you know it?" I asked.

"I grew up in LaCrosse," she exclaimed, her eyes widening in amazement. I asked if she knew our friends Curt and Lyla, with whom we'd had supper in Valparaiso.

"I think I went to high school with their daughter" she said, her voice rising an octave.

We shared more about traveling, coffee, and their suggestions on which shops to visit when we got to Missoula, remarking on how small the world truly is.

Coffee shops stocked with the beloved roasted beans of wholesalers like Andy and Sara's Blue Mind Coffee Roasters of Indianapolis are essential refuges for bicycle touring. Though we appreciate the ubiquitous presence and consistent goods of Starbucks, Marriotts, Caseys, and Walmart, and we appreciate more the independence, tenacity, and unique vibe of independent coffee shops, booksellers, B&Bs, and roadside produce stands. These self-determining sanctuaries seem to be holding out against the corporate mega-retailers that screech cookie-cutter facades, products, and colors from Woonsocket, Rhode Island, to Walnut Creek, California.

I contemplated what a cross-country ride arranged on only using these independent purveyors would be like. Could it even be done? Would it demonstrate that there remains autonomous places in America that reflect a region's cultural context and historical values instead of company branding, cash flow, and stockholder value? I was sure we could add small-town diners to the list, and we'd enjoy unique aromas, ambiance, intellectual stimulus, and food without ever needing to step into a place that is the same regardless if you are walking through the door in Manhattan, New York or Lima, Peru.

———

After the weeks of bicycling the dry plains of South Dakota and Eastern Wyoming, the shift to green, water-filled meadows, evergreen trees, and woodland we encountered within ten miles of leaving Buffalo was startling. About two miles out of town as RT 16 began its steep grade up the over 6,100-foot elevation gain to Powder River Pass, we came upon a road crew clearing trees on the hillside.

"Hey, where you heading?" one of the crew called out.

"Ten Sleep," I breathlessly replied.

"All today?" he asked.

"South Fork Lodge overnight, Ten Sleep tomorrow," I croaked out.

"We're heading up there in a few minutes. Throw the bikes in the truck, and I'll give you a lift," was his warm and welcoming reply.

In everyone's life there come times of temptation in the wilderness. I knew in an instant, this was one of mine. Not one person would need to know if I loaded my bike and gasping lungs into that pickup truck. Cheryl would be fine with it; her "I don't have anything to prove" mindset wouldn't even be inclined to think it a black mark on our expedition. I told myself I would still ride the gain tomorrow up to Powder River Pass, legitimizing our Rocky Mountain crossing with the ride to 9,666 feet even if I did do the first half of it in the bed of a pickup at forty-five miles per hour instead of the three and a half I was now averaging.

I smiled at the young man and pedaled on, thinking, "Get behind me, you Lucifer, you."

South Fork Lodge is a beautiful rustic camp of log cabins and restaurants nestled on the edge of gurgling South Clear Creek. Our climb of eighteen miles and 3,300 feet of elevation gain progressed slowly, cloaked with sweat and frequent breaks to stand awestruck at the views of snowcapped mountains, green hills, and high meadow streams running in all directions. We would catch our breaths and be in awe of how quickly the parched rolling mounds of South Dakota and eastern Wyoming had morphed into lushness.

In our second "It's a small world, Mickey Mouse" moment in two days, we discovered a hometown connection with South Fork Lodge. After arriving and checking into an adorable cabin on the side of South Clear Creek, we went down to the rustic log cabin restaurant and office to eat and use the internet. I posted a picture of our bikes up against the hitching post railing on Instagram and remarked on how welcoming South Fork was. Within minutes, a friend posted a comment that she and her husband had eaten at South Fork a few times, and the cook there was from our hometown.

"Really, who?" I quickly typed.

"We can't remember his name," she posted in return.

The truth is, I really wanted to know who she was talking about. Cheryl and I talked about how to find out. The lodge was run by a very young and very capable group of women—less than twenty years old, by our guess—so we figured they wouldn't know but asked anyway.

"Say, do you know if your cook is from Connecticut?"

"I don't think so; he's from Buffalo."

"Do you know if there once was a cook here from Connecticut?"

"Not sure. The owner will be here at breakfast. She might know."

I thought about posting again, and when I looked at my Instagram account I saw another comment from yet another friend letting me know who that cook was.

"Yes, that's his name," our first commenter validated.

It turns out this cook had been a few years ahead of us in high school. I remembered him well because he was President of the Ski Club and treated me well during my freshman year, a time of doubt and insecurity that can be reduced with simple acceptance and respect from someone four years older.

Next morning, all was confirmed as we ate breakfast at the counter where we met Holi, owner of South Fork. Cheryl asked, "We were wondering, did you used to have a cook here from Ellington, Connecticut?"

"Sure did. Actually, he's coming back next month. He would've been here all summer but has been taking care of grandkids because of Covid, and he needed to help his family during the summer break."

Pedaling from the driveway and turning right back onto Rt 16 for the more than 3,000-feet of elevation gain to Powder River Pass, I thought, wow, how small the world is.

We arrived at Powder River Pass before 2 PM and experienced the dopamine effect you get when something once feared turns out to be a thrill. I stood our bikes next to the sign, and we could hardly believe all the worry, anxiety, and raw fear about age and ability had melted away like the snow piles around us running into small rivulets of water.

Cheryl, however, hadn't dispatched all her worries. She is not a fan of fast downhills on a bicycle, and we were now going to plunge

5,240 feet into the town of Ten Sleep in just twenty-eight miles. Pure fun for me; raw fear for her.

Cheryl rode first and set the pace, and we headed past our first marker, the Leigh Creek RV dump station, where signs clearly command: No Camping. Really? No kidding. We gained speed and encountered light traffic giving us freedom to "take the road," riding in the middle of the right-hand traffic lane. The downhill in these first miles was surrounded by sweeping views of high meadows, evergreen woods, and mountain pastures lined by split-rail fencing. The road was in great condition with wide shoulders and well-cared-for gravel-lined culverts to channel melting snow and rain-water off the road.

The wind was in our faces. Actually, we were going fast now and creating wind in our faces. My heart rate was fine, but I guessed Cheryl was hitting close to her red zone. Going downhill fast is not her riding style. Yet, she was riding with confidence as we passed the Meadowlark Lodge and Ski area. A long, wide, hairpin turn at the north end of Meadow Lark Lake swept us southwest into increasing steepness as we headed toward Deer Haven Lodge and Boulder Park Campground.

Ten Sleep Creek was on our right now and joined us for the twenty-eight-mile descent into Ten Sleep Canyon. Soon, it crossed under the road and was on our left as the topography around us began to change. This switching right and left, with the creek moving back and forth on each side of the road, increased our sense of speed. I looked down at my speedometer, amazed to see us hitting over twenty-five miles per hour. No need for me to worry about my partner's hesitation.

The meadows and trees ebbed away to gravel, soil, and boulder-strewn outcroppings. The horizon in front of us became a narrowing valley with high cliff walls on our left as the creek continued on the right. We were entering Ten Sleep Canyon, and the road steepened. A pull off named Vista Point offered a bird's view of two hairpin turns to come. Staying in the middle of the road, we rounded the hairpins, centrifugal force pulling us into the opposite. We were mesmerized by the sheer beauty of the day and electrified by our speed and the sound of wind rushing through our helmets. Everything had come together to make one of our most feared experiences morph into an experience I hope never to forget. Thrilling is too low-calorie a word to attach to those two hours.

Popping out of the canyon, the terrain leveled into a valley, and we coasted into the village of Ten Sleep, population 206. Named by trappers using the Native American Peoples method of using distance to name locations, Ten Sleep is ten nights from Yellowstone Valley and ten nights from a camp on the Laramie River, now the present-day city of Laramie. Ten Sleep has a colorful history of conflict, but today is home to a broad mix of fishermen, rock climbers, horsemen, and hunters. It's an eclectic place where you'll find a rough and dark storefront bar next to a coffee shop that you imagined was plucked from downtown San Francisco.

———

The next ten days were a series of high desert small towns punctuated by some larger settlements and a couple of small cities. We crossed the Big Horn River at Menderson where we also cycled back onto US Route 20, that ribbon of asphalt that, like us, started in Boston. Route 20 runs almost directly north at this point through the town of Basin and into Greybull where we spent the night in a beautiful and historic hotel.

The following day, as we headed toward the town of Lovell, we experienced two events that weeks earlier would have been unnerving, and although we felt some of that discomfort, it was now accompanied by a sense of thrill.

Knowing we only had thirty-four miles to Greybull, we ignored my oft-repeated mantra to start early and end early. We departed around mid-day on the ever-present Route 14 towards Cody. Because we were skirting around Yellowstone, we soon turned north on US Route 310, leaving the ACA Parks, Peaks, and Prairies mapped route and riding onto a route of our own selection. Route 310 undulates in a series of ups and downs, bordered by dry grass turned a yellowish burnt sienna by the drought. Cattle were loosely scattered in the gullies and ditches along the roadside finding what shade and green grasses they could, and traffic was light as the day turned hot.

Off to our left, we could see dark clouds and a lowering sky, and with winds moving across our left shoulder, it was clear this squall was taking aim at us. As it came closer, the winds increased, and though we could not hear thunder, we saw lightning—long jagged streaks of light extending from those dark clouds to what appeared to be the ground a mile or two away.

I couldn't communicate with Cheryl, but I sensed she sped up, which told me she saw this amazing display playing out as well. I looked around and saw places as we passed by, now at a fast fourteen or more miles per hour, that we might be able to find cover in. Culverts, a few with big pipes to divert water in flash floods, appeared at the little valleys of those rolling hills. The problem was evident, too; the cattle were not loosely scattered around the hills any longer. They had moved into those culverts and pipe tunnels, and although I couldn't see any bulls in the group, I was not hopeful they would share space with two humans with steel bicycles when the storm blew in.

The wind had picked up; we could hear thunder now almost in unison with lightning. I pulled up next to Cheryl, waved my arm, and shouted, "Go, move fast; we need to outrun this, and don't wait for me; just go."

I think it was the only time she used the turbo option on her e-assist and moved. Fast.

The thing is, I was smiling. It was a magnificent display of nature and power. Fear was minimal as I was fairly confident we could outrun this. This storm was a dry thunderstorm, frequent in the west during summers of drought, so we were not destined to get wet. These storms are raucous, fast moving, can cause wildfires, and have clearly defined borders. I could see the dark line of that storm pass behind me within a hundred yards.

As it passed behind us, we pulled over.

"That was amazing," Cheryl said, eyes open wide as I rolled up next to her.

"Thrilling," I answered. And it was. The storm, now off to our right, headed east while we continued on toward Lovell.

By 2:30 PM, the temperature had passed ninety, the Wyoming landscape offered no shade, and we sweated as if sitting in some spa's steam room. Until we didn't. You stop sweating when dehydrated, which stops your body from cooling itself, which can become dangerous if not responded to. We only had eight miles to go to the next town, so I wasn't concerned. Then I noticed a wobble and a feeling through the bike that clearly wasn't right. My first flat tire since leaving Buffalo, New York. The back tire, of course, always more difficult to deal with.

You can outrun a thunderstorm, but you cannot outpace the Wyoming heat. There was no shade anywhere and the heat intensified as I unhooked the paniers, flipped the bike over on its seat and handlebars, and disconnected the wheel from the frame and gear cassette. After pulling off the tire, I was able to find the source of the puncture, but as persistent as I was, I could not get a patch to stick to the punctured tube due to the heat and its softening effect on the rubber.

Normally, this would be fine because I never rode five miles at home without carrying a spare tube. But I had mistakenly thrown our extra inner tubes into the bounce box we used to send packages ahead when we didn't think we'd need tents or winter clothes. This box was waiting for us in Bozeman a week away. Then it hit me.

This was it, the moment I questioned after changing that flat tie in a Mobile gas station back in Schenectady. What would we do in the middle of nowhere, thousands of miles from home, if we broke down? I was living the big fear I had early in the ride and was not finding a solution.

Now closing in on 5 PM with a depleted water supply, I suggested Cheryl ride ahead to our hotel and I would hitchhike a ride into town. This is not her comfort zone, and knowing she would imagine everything from me being kidnapped to being flattened by a semi-trailer, I happily told her not to panic or worry. Which is akin to asking her not to sweat. She reluctantly started riding, and I stuck out my thumb while walking aside, not astride, my loaded bike.

Although traffic was light, within ten minutes a pickup truck passed, made a U-turn, and asked if I needed help. After explaining our situation, my Mennonite rescuers helped me load my steel steed and panniers into the bed of their truck and drove me to the Travelodge on the east side of Lovell just as Cheryl was dismounting her bike and heading to check in.

We left Lovell later than desired so we could wait for Hardware Hank to open and buy a few inner tubes to carry with us. Given our record so far, we were not expecting to need them, but just in case, we purchased three.

Just in case came north of the tiny burg of Frannie, yards before the Montana border. Not one of us, but both of us within feet of each other, had back tires punctured by a nail and knife-sharp rock. It was as if Montana didn't want us or Wyoming wanted to keep us.

We laughed. Now, with tubes, new patches, and temperatures only in the eighties, we fixed the flats and pedaled happily over Sage Creek. As we entered our twelfth state, we stopped at the Welcome to Montana sign for a picture.

SIXTEEN

Hitting the Wall

Montana

We spent a night in Bridger at a motel common in these locations. Paneled walls, pink porcelain tubs and sinks, with window shades that sound like soda cans rattling on the floor in the back seat of a car crossing railroad tracks when you raise and lower them. The air conditioner blew loudly and pumped out a lukewarm breeze on our heads at night.

But Bridger was also a point of delineation. We were riding north now along the Clarks Fork of the Yellowstone River. Topography and vegetation were changing as we approached Rockvale and moved into Joliet, where we came on our first drive-through coffee shack that would prove to be common in the Northwest.

The next twenty miles offered drastic change as we left the high desert landscape and descended into the lush green Yellowstone River Valley and the town of Columbus. Turning west we once again started an on-again, off-again dance with I-90 as we alternated riding on the behemoth of an interstate's fourteen-foot shoulder with a parallel frontage road that appeared and disappeared as the surrounding hills and the rushing Yellowstone River allowed.

Reeds Point is a small river town of less than 250 residents about twenty miles from Columbus, cushioned on the banks of the Yellowstone River. It is a sheep town and home to the Great Montana Sheep Drive, held annually on Memorial Day. We entered town on Division Street and found the Valley Farmer's Supply at the corner of Division and Central Ave. A three-pump, single-bay Cenex gas station and convenience store, were businesses housed together in a single-story, free-standing white and red metal building with a stone façade running like a skirt around the outside. This was our kind of place for lunch. This entrepreneurial menage faced east with the local post office and the neat-as-a-pin Old West RV Park across the street.

Reeds Point was the type of town I would live in if I moved to the area. As we passed the Painted Lady Bed & Breakfast heading out of town, Paula came running down the street after us.

"Hello, where are you guys going?"

"Well tonight we are heading to Livingston, eventually the Pacific."

"That is so neat. Amazing, really, where did you start?"

When I explained Boston and our plans, she became even more animated and friendly.

"Tell me about Reeds Point; has this always been home for you?" I asked shifting the conversation.

"No, not many people are actually from here," she explained.

"It looks to me as if Reeds Point is thriving. Are people moving in as Livingston grows?"

"Yes, we love this place and it's growing. The RV park, great public fishing access to the river, local B&Bs, and taverns are all doing well."

We talked some more about the annual sheep drive, the high cost of living in Livingston, and the influence of nearby Paradise Valley, a region occupied by the celebrities and the uber-wealthy. Wishing each other well, I thought how and why people randomly approach us.

If we were riding bicycles that did not have panniers strapped to the sides bulging with our gear, I do not believe Paula would have come running after us to see what we were about. But those bags speak to something inside of people that breaks past barriers of reluctance to approach strangers.

Do we do this with our attitude or how we carry ourselves emotionally? Are there ways we pull people towards provoking curiosity and interest?

I think many people who approached us saw something hopeful in the fact that two ordinary people, now over sixty, would or could ride a bicycle loaded up for long-distance travel. They may not want to ride a bike across the country, but most of them referenced a dream of their own and were intrigued when they saw us attempting to make ours happen. We bid goodbye to Paula and headed west towards a night in Big Timber followed by a short day into the small city of Livingston, population approximately 8,000.

We had been to Livingston two years earlier, and it was terrific to pedal into this small metropolis bustling with RVs, local ranchers, and cowboy wannabes. I mentioned to Cheryl that it was like California in Montana. Its trendy restaurants and stores of chic Western fashion with New York labels seemed more suitable to Santa Monica than a mountain range. I suspect it is more evidence of the Paradise Valley population of actors and Silicon Valley tycoons.

I fell asleep that night in Livingston wondering about the next day's climb over Bozeman Pass into Bozeman. We were going to be riding on I-90 yet again, and my recollection of the ride from our previous trip was that it was a long steep climb followed by a sharp and winding downhill. My memory would prove accurate on both points.

————

Our climb towards Bozeman started as nice as could be. It was a cool, sun-filled morning and presented a bonus of no headwind.

I was philosophical this morning, prompted by a sense that we were approaching the downhill side of this whole journey and aided by an unconscious awareness that wildfires dressing the air in murky smoke were a premonition. I started to think about this as an allegory to life. Riding up the slope towards a conclusion, a transition that was so long anticipated. It felt like a foreboding sense that life itself is no longer given to the expected and hoped for, but to be completed. A poem came to me in a flash as I rode up to Bozeman Pass.

> Traveling the River valley
> In the early morning sun
> Wondering what had gotten him this far
> And from what he had to run
>
> The haze of fires behind - or is it ahead
> Clouds the azure - speaking grey instead

I thought I would title it "Ambiguity."

———

We reached Bozeman Pass before 8:50 AM and googled to see what the elevation was; I found a live webcam at this 5,702-foot mountain gap. I texted family and friends to go online, and we waved to them in real time. I'm not sure why it felt like a special connection at that moment, but it did.

But the idyllic ride quickly morphed into a white-knuckle descent. We cycled on frontage and gravel roads aside I-90 and passed the Montana Grizzly Encounter, where our only option was to climb the entrance ramp and alongside the seventy-mile-per-hour traffic heading down the snakelike turns of the interstate as it hurdled into Bozeman. So far, riding I-90 has not been overly alarming. Wide shoulders gave us a sense of space, and drivers were alert to our presence, often moving left to give us even more room. Not today. This section of the highway is narrow; shoulders felt half of the typical fourteen feet, and they were strewn with shredded tires, sand, and litter. Traffic was being pressed and squeezed together, which seemed to be about an arm's length or less away. It was a terrifying eight miles.

Our time in Bozeman, including a day off, was a respite, though. We stayed at a familiar hotel, ate in a familiar restaurant, walked roads we'd perambulated in the past, and best of all, connected with friends who happened to be traveling through Montana on a cross-country RV trip. Tom and LaNae, with their kids, Tim, Bethany and Michael, met us, fed us, and just gave us a sense of belonging which long-time traveling pickpockets from you.

Maybe it was reconnecting with this wonderful family, maybe it was the scary eight miles into town, maybe it was the smoke or the recognition of being more than two-thirds of our way across the country, but I was introspective now.

I had changed over the past twelve months. Hurts from people and organizations, disappointment with choices others made that seemed selfish and short-sighted, and an inner sense to move into a creative period of life all fused to form a few days of looking at the past and how they might point toward some future. I could see those negatives with an emotional distance I don't believe would be the same had we not ridden over two thousand miles.

I thought of the Biblical verse in Jeremiah that urges you to stand in the ways, see and ask for the old path, the good way, and walk in them if you wish for inner rest.

I thought about a section of the book *The Heart Aroused and the Preservation of the Soul in Corporate America,* written by Poet David Whyte, on lessons at life junctions. I don't remember them exactly, but they ruminated in my thoughts as:

Don't leave the old path for a new one.

Don't judge another person's behavior.

Save your anger for another day.

––––––––

Leaving Bozeman, we spent the next night at the Sportsman Inn in Ennis. Ennis brings us onto the official Adventure Cycling Association Trans America Route, the route of the 1976 Bikecentennial. It had been this ride I long ago thought about traversing the US, and although I doubted I would ever pedal the entire TransAm, it gave me a wistful feeling to at least cycle a section of it.

Ennis to Virginia City is fifteen miles. The first twelve miles involves a steady climb of 2,000 feet in elevation, followed by a glorious downhill run of 1,000 feet over the last three miles. It was a fun morning. Virginia City is a jumble of historical sights and events involving the Crow Nation conflicts, prospectors mining for gold sprouting a boom town, that town busting into a ghost town, lawless robbers and outlaws, and a town daughter who became the first lady of the Confederacy. By the middle of the last century, it had fallen into busted status again, and in the 1960s, the National Park Service and the State of Montana joined forces to restore the town's richness, renovating it like a Western movie set for tourism.

———

By the morning we left Ennis we were in a remarkably different mindset than we were early in our ride. In the first weeks, mornings were accompanied by a measure of apprehension about the weather, road conditions, route finding, alertness for problems, and anxiety to get to our destination each afternoon. Now, we were relaxed, almost nonchalant on leaving each morning, easy to stop along the way and visit with others, and we took time to ponder the past in our literal and proverbial rearview mirrors. We were confident each morning about the day ahead, but also about finishing the journey. It was starting to feel reachable. Little did I know as we headed toward lunch in Virginia City that our relaxed ride and anxiety-free mood were just hours away from disappearing in one sentence uttered by a happy diner owner putting our meal down on the table.

"You can't go past Twin Bridges; the roads into Sula are all shut down to everyone except firefighters."

> "There is a book of Revelation in every one's life, as there is in the Bible."
>
> Anne Shirley, *Anne of Green Gables*

It was here that our cheery waitress informed us of the online wildfire map that would send currents of anxiety jolting through me like lightning. And it was here that an entirely new route and schedule to the Pacific Ocean started to take shape.

The sense of dread and regret which culminated in dissonant voices of self-blame early the next morning in Twin Bridges began slowly in Virginia City, like the early winds of a hurricane. Those inner demons were just starting to gather as we left lunch, and I intuitively sensed something was about to shift dramatically.

I've had other times like this: job loss due to company mergers, people who've proven to be false friends, and disappointments that prompted raw self-evaluation of my choices and motives. They start slow, build fast, and overtake you like the 18-wheelers we've shared the road with over the past 2,800 miles: noisy with punishing wind that sucks you in and pushes you over, all at once.

Riding now into Missoula with Gail, my mind yelling at her to drive and be quiet, I held conflicting ideas in my mind: we have succeeded with 2,500 miles pedaled, no accidents, and tens of thousands of pedal strokes without harm or breakage. But we have failed, and I was convinced that I'd never get back here to finish. Even if I did, it would not be the same.

We made the best of our time in Missoula. One of our first stops in town was the Adventure Cycling Association Headquarters located downtown in a converted church. ACA headquarters are a pilgrimage for bicycle tourers passing through Missoula, and as we walked through the doors, Greg Siple, ACA founder and original organizer of the 1976 Bikecentenial, walked in with us. We couldn't have planned that.

Although retired, Greg continues to be a presence in the ACA community. He introduced himself, asked about our ride, and when I used my visit to register as a lifelong member of the Association, Greg was kind enough to sign and draw a picture for us on our copy of the book *America's Bicycle Route: The Story of the Transamerica Bicycle Trail* by Michael McCoy and Greg Siple. This is a beautiful hardcover book given to every lifetime member as a gift for their commitment and contribution to the organization.

We enjoyed the upscale coffee shops and trendy restaurants for a day, but it was now arrangements, not miles, we had to focus on. Find a bike shop, pay to pack bicycles up, and then coordinate getting them shipped back to Connecticut. When I get home, I'll play it with nonchalance. I knew all the things to say and had this script running in my head:

Yeah, wildfires shut out our routes, we came home, still did over 2,300 miles, saw lots of great places, met wonderful people everywhere. It's fine, no big deal. Sure, right, we'll finish next year. Although I did not really think we would.

I had a different script running in my thoughts. It went like:

"This is a first-world problem. Get over yourself. It's the journey, not the destination."

"So many worse things could have happened. This is nothing."

" Blah. Blah. Blah."

These thoughts made me want to puke.

It really was not about the miles but about the portage of carrying sixty years of life into the next last phase. How do you explain that if you don't make the other shore?

PART VI
Missoula to Pacific City

SEVENTEEN

Dreams Redux

Be patient; It is the action before the act.

As we cycled out of Missoula and headed towards Idaho, I was more in awe of the fact we were riding again than I was of the beautiful Clark's Fork River Valley and surrounding mountains. Probably the river and hills being obscured by a smokey blue haze had something to do with it, too.

It hadn't ended after all. On August 4th, after more than a week off the bikes and hourly views of the online fire map, it was clear fires in some parts of Montana were becoming contained.

The I-90 corridor from Missoula to Spokane wasn't as menacing to cycle through as it had been weeks earlier, so we decided to return and finish.

It was August 10th. As we left home, I thought of the plan: to get up early enough, check luggage, switch planes in Chicago, catch the connector to Missoula, have all bags make the connections, Uber to the bike shop, and get the bikes. Everything would need to work almost flawlessly.

And it did.

We were early enough to check into our downtown Missoula hotel, enjoy a relaxing evening, and talk about how incredible it was to be back here.

I wasn't naïve. I knew these next fifteen days were a gift. We needed to enjoy it. Be. Flexible. Resist the urge just to get it done. It reminded me of the idea of not rushing into retirement but to take time to relive and enjoy memories of past triumphs, trials, and friends.

I also knew getting back on the bike after two weeks would be hard. It would be hot; it's the West, in August, during a drought. We would need to stay strong physically and mentally, all while being gentle with ourselves. I knew there would still be disappointments like smoke, heat, hills, and wind. Of course, that wind. But, hey, that is life, and we were energized anew to sit with the challenges and move.

But truthfully, instead of hard, hot, smoke, hills, and disappointment, I was thinking about how these last days would be unique. Let's face it; the fires have made for a better story. We would ride through the Clark Fork Valley overshadowed by the Bitterroot Mountains, if we could only see them, and we would cycle on some of America's premier bicycle paths.

Our new plans included a ride through the Palouse region, an area we'll see for the first time. We would visit beautiful towns like Harrison and Moscow, Idaho, and pedal along America's fourth-largest river, the Columbia. We would cycle the Columbia River Gorge Historic Roadway, a car-free road patterned after the great highways of Europe.

We would run our front tires into the Pacific Ocean together just days after our forty-fifth wedding anniversary.

What lessons the last weeks had taught. Despair turned back to expectation promising a fulfilled dream sweeter than ever.

It was a fantastic ride through Missoula; the smoke had eased since we were there two weeks earlier, and the flowers exploding in the ever-present boxes and gardens seemed to be as delighted with the cleansed air as we were.

We rode onto an unexpected bike path that eventually turned into the Frenchtown Frontage Road. A lightly trafficked road running yards north of I-90 gave us the benefits of the interstate's mellower topography without the noise and hurtling traffic. By 2 PM, we were in Alberton, our stop for the night at the River Edge Resort and Steakhouse.

While riding that first day back, a favorite poem came to mind as a metaphor for our last three weeks.

LOST

Stand still. The trees ahead and bushes beside you
Are not lost. Wherever you are is called Here,
And you must treat it as a powerful stranger,
Must ask permission to know it and be known.
The forest breathes. Listen. It answers,
I have made this place around you.
If you leave it, you may come back again, saying
    Here.
No two trees are the same to Raven.
No two branches are the same to Wren.
If what a tree or a bush does is lost on you,
You are surely lost. Stand still. The forest knows
Where you are. You must let it find you.

David Wagoner

I was touched by the sense that we had been found or that the dream had found us, and I was not lost. I needed to stand still and seek, then ask and receive permission to be back here, less sure than any road we had been on since we began. Wow, what an allegory for our life right now.

With little planning, we were in for a week of unknown roads and experiences. I hadn't had time to research this route, check out Google Street View, or do more than see if campgrounds or hotels existed on the Clark's Fork River corridor. A river valley running from Spokane, Washington, to Missoula is the passageway for what has become our ever-present chum, Interstate 90.

The serendipitous nature of this change wasn't lost on me, either. Originally, I had planned everything from the various roads, overnights, and elevation gained and lost from the first mile to our expected last. The wall of wildfires along Idaho Route 12 through the Lolo Wilderness turned us northwest. We were going to figure it out as we went. No real plans, no spreadsheet either, for these last days and miles.

This might be an excellent way to approach this final phase of our lives as much as it was to ride the final phase of our cycle across the continent. It can be tempting to move into a significant life transition with a need to control, plan extensively about the future, and avoid past mistakes and disappointments.

But a disruptive change can be energy for grabbing onto new experiences. That is what we were doing. The lesson here was to do that for the next thirty miles and the next thirty years.

———

It didn't take long for us to hit our first unplanned contest. Riding out of Alberton, we picked up the frontage road for a few miles. It ended abruptly at the entrance ramp to I-90, and we rode for about five miles on the behemoth's shoulder. Jumping off at the opportunity, we found ourselves on a gravel road climbing the side of a sharp hillside. Both the interstate and the river were on our left.

This gravel-grinding section was unexpected and delightful. Until it wasn't. Soon the gravel regressed into dirt, which degenerated into a single track more akin to a hiking trail. Bikepacking is the latest iteration of bicycle travel, and this section gave us a taste of what this more adventurous cousin of bike touring is like. But we were not really set up for it, and I was glad that Lady Google disclosed we had about two more miles to go and we'd hit a small road leading us back onto another frontage road.

But not before we hit a couple of detours. We were obviously on an old railroad bed, and standing in front of us was an old tunnel with a once majestic entrance now closed halfway by a pile of rocks. At first look, it was clear we should not, would not, pass through this. Everything from snakes, spiders, outlaws, and falling rocks filled our imaginations. A scarcely visible path led off to our left and a few minutes of scouting disclosed we could walk the bikes up and around to the other side.

After admiring the work of Alberton's graffiti artists, who lined the tunnel walls, we hiked the bikes around to the west side entrance. Partially blocked by a pile of boulders, the tunnel entrance framed the 200-foot dark passage in a striking contrast of dark and light.

Continuing our walk west, just as the road improved enough to ride again, we faced obstacle number two. There, warning us with signs not to cross this property, was a barbed wire fence clearly meant to tell us to turn around.

The next few minutes were a humorous microcosm of our different personality types. For Cheryl, there was one answer. Turn around, pedal back the seven miles we've just rode, and find another way. For me, that wasn't even a possibility. So, a short discussion followed with Cheryl presenting the rational, and I the inventive.

"We can't do this; it's trespassing."

"I think it's really meant for ATVs, which rip up property."

"We're in Montana; this is someone's property. We've seen some people carrying guns around here, remember."

This reasoning gave me pause, and for a microsecond, I thought about riding the seven miles back east. Only for a microsecond, though, before I retorted, "Here, take off your panniers," unclip-ping my own and setting them on the other side of the barbed wire.

"I don't know," Cheryl replied but slowly unclipped her own while I held the strands apart for her to step over and under to the trespassing side of this predicament.

Passing the last of the bags through, I lifted Cheryl's bike up and over the fence, eyes searching the hills behind her for any angry Montanans.

After heaving my own bike over, Cheryl held the wires apart for me; she was now clearly part of this criminal act.

"Let's hope any nearby landowners are late sleepers. We have just a mile to ride, and Lady Google says we'll come out on Mead Lane, which leads to Old Highway 10. It looks like we can continue riding that for a long way. Let's go!" I said with a bit of unease in my voice.

Popping out onto Mead Lane with relief and a jolt of excitement with the feeling we'd just gotten away with something, we passed into the little town of Superior without incident.

Later I learned that our tunnel is the abandoned Cyr #18 Tunnel on what was once the Chicago Milwaukee, St. Paul & Pacific Railroad. Built in 1908, the tunnel is officially a derelict and abandoned part of the old line that ran through this Alberton and Sawmill Gorge and may have been used up to the 1980s. One comment on my internet investigation caught my eye: "Watch out for rattlesnakes." Had that information been available as we stood at the east entrance before walking our bikes around the two-hundred-and-fifty-two-foot tunnel, Cheryl would have instantly turned around and pedaled furiously back east before I had time to argue. I would have been inclined to catch her.

Riding on Old Highway 10 we felt like kids who'd just gotten away with stealing cookies out of the proverbial jar. We would never have chosen this route if we had planned these next three weeks like the first two months. Meaning that we would never have found a deteriorating gravel track or derelict train tunnel or had the opportunity to stealth ride our way out of posted land.

It wouldn't be the last unforeseen adventure up the Clark River Valley.

Riding into St. Regis for a night at the Super 8, we traveled a beautifully paved, lightly traveled road. Smoke increased as the day wore on, and for a while we pedaled next to trees which showed signs of past fires through the area. The ground around these evergreens was cleared and painted with bright light green grass spreading out like a shag carpet. It was an explosion of young life. The bark of each tree, however, told a story. They were veined with black edges encircling each little cell of bark about twenty or more feet up the tree. The trees were stripped of lower branches, and although the contrast of black to sienna bark against the chartreuse grasses was otherworldly, it was clear this was the remnant of past fires that had swept across this road. It was new life springing phoenix-like, enclosing old and stubborn trunks determined to hang on and survive.

I pondered, was that me trying to find another gasp for life before the next fire came and took more than I could recover from? Am I riding across this country looking like these old beat-up trees surrounded by bright and vibrant life that should be taking over? It could be, but like these old, scarred trees, I didn't care; I was hanging on, too.

———

Mornings were cold, and I assume it was because we were at 2,700 feet of elevation. We headed towards Wallace, Idaho, on the Olympian Rail Trail Route. This thirty-mile section of the old Pacific Route of the Milwaukee Railroad seemed to run up the valley parallel to I-90, but I had not researched it much, given our change in plans after Missoula.

It was soon to show itself to be more of a gravel and bike-packing track than a bike-touring route. We rode rough and single-track grass paths until we hit a section washed out in a flood along Two Mile Creek. It was too steep and dangerous to descend and cross the creek, so we backtracked to Two Mile Road and onto the interstate on-ramp, assuming we'd need to ride at least ten miles to the next exit.

Once again, the unexpected turned into the serendipitous. Climbing the ramp onto I-90 West, we found all traffic had been diverted to the southbound lanes, and I-90 heading north towards Spokane was empty and cleaned ready for repaving.

We hesitated at first, not knowing if we'd be turned around by construction or a bridge inaccessible to this lane. But without much of an option, we proceeded and rode the next twelve miles to De Borgia where we could pick up the Route of the Olympian again.

As we were about to leave the highway at De Borgia, we came on a workman sitting in his pickup, apparently waiting for I don't know what or whom. We asked him how much longer we would have the road to ourselves.

"Couple of miles," he responded without welcome or disdain.

"I'm assuming we're okay to have jumped on here then. The bike trail was washed out back at the creek and it sure was nice to find this empty," I replied, trying to sound friendly and nonchalant at the same time.

"Sure, you're not the first cyclists to pass by here for sure. Enjoy." A slight smile poked the corners of his mouth. Maybe.

The Route of the Olympian started to climb and, according to descriptions, would at some point connect to the Route of the Hiawatha, a popular tourist trail on the border of Montana and Idaho. This trail is fifteen miles long, passes through ten tunnels, and has a complete infrastructure of vendors to shuttle you to the top, so all you need to ride is the descent.

We didn't do it. Yes, I regret that.

Soon, we found ourselves back on I-90 at the Dana Mora Rest Stop, taking a respite before climbing five miles to Lookout Pass, the Montana and Idaho border, and a descent of five miles into Mullen, Idaho.

We met Paul and Kris there. They were about our age, happy, inquisitive, and friendly. Paul asked about our trip, and when I mentioned we were headed to Pacific City, Oregon, he about jumped up and down.

"My wife, Kris, she's inside the rest area. She was just there last week with a bunch of her girlfriends."

Turns out Paul and Kris are newlyweds, well, almost. Married just two years, Kris was from Portland, and Paul from Helena, Montana, where they lived now. I was sure there was a story there, but he didn't share, and I didn't ask.

When Kris showed up, she showed us pictures from Pacific City and shared that she had lived in Los Angeles and at various places along the west coast up to Portland over the years.

"I'm a West Coast Girl," she stated with no little pride. Definitely a story here, I thought to myself.

"Do you miss Portland?" I asked.

"No, it's been destroyed by the last administration. I was so fortunate to have lived there during a Golden Age, but after visiting recently, I never need to go back," she offered, now with a hint of melancholy.

We spent about thirty to forty minutes visiting with Paul and Kris, talking about Montana, camping, and the similarities between Asheville, North Carolina, and Portland, Oregon, before 2016. They offered good information about peddling the upcoming Trail of The Coeur d'Alene and Wallace, Idaho, places they seemed to know well.

Something else happened with Kris and Paul. It was small, yet something of a point of transition. When Kris started to tell us about Pacific City, she spoke in the positive.

"You will love Pacific City. It is so picturesque – a great place to complete your trip. There are great restaurants, and you should go to Pelican Brewing. It's the one right on the beach in front of the big rock."

I am not a person given to premonitions, but Kris didn't say, "If you get there." She talked about when we got there as if there was no doubt about it. She sounded like she was talking to someone who was a mile away and driving in a car. It was a sure thing, not an out-there possibility. It gave me an internal gasp of emotion. For a second, it was no longer "believing" we would make it to the Pacific; it was a certainty. An absolute. Her words were the evidence of something we'd not yet seen. It was like something accomplished, yet still to come. Faith into reality.

EIGHTEEN

Synchronicity

Idaho

Not long after saying goodbye to Kris and Paul, we climbed over Lookout Pass on I-90. At 4,710 feet, it marks the border between Idaho and Montana, between Mountain and Pacific Time Zones, and our thirteenth state. We gained another instantaneous hour to the day as we started the long descent toward Wallace, Idaho. About a mile into the downhill, we stopped to read a historic marker describing the devastating effects of a 1910 fire that ravaged the area. Over three million acres were burned, and eighty-five lives were lost in this area that year. Like this summer, smoke from this fire impacted cities such as Boston and New York. It gave me a small chill. We are small compared to the forces of the natural world.

We soon exited the highway in the little town of Mullen. This was a well-ordered place of just over 600 people with a high school, Sinclair Gas Station, and the expected one motel, café, and bar and grill.

Yet, Mullen was important. It is the terminus for the Trail of the Coeur d'Alenes. The Idaho State website describes this trail well:

The Trail of the Coeur d'Alenes is a 73-mile paved trail spanning the Idaho panhandle between Mullan and Plummer. It was created through a unique partnership between the Coeur d'Alene Tribe, Union Pacific Railroad, the U. S. Government, and the State of Idaho. The trail meanders through the historic Silver Valley, along the Coeur d'Alene River past scenic Lake Coeur d'Alene and through rolling farmlands to Plummer.

It is beautiful and ranks at the top of all the bicycle trails we have traveled on. It was rivaled only by the upcoming Historic Columbia River State Trail in Oregon and slightly ahead of the Elroy Sparta Trail, which we rode what seemed like many, many weeks ago.

It was also fitting as it followed our final juxtaposition from the noise and frenzied traffic on I-90 into the gentle, quiet, and nature-filled miles of this trail. It was monumental and welcomed.

———

Our next two-and-a-half days on the Trail of the Coeur d'Alenes were amiable in every way possible. Wallace, seven miles from Mullen, welcomed us with a street fair offering live music, art, street performers, and huckleberry ice cream. We had hit the annual Wallace Huckleberry Festival and everything huckleberry would seem to follow us for the next two weeks. It became apparent the Pacific Northwest revels in its love of this native berry. Although they have a similar appearance to blueberries, this native plant has a different taste and color when ripe.

Native American tribes were known to have held ceremonies to collect these berries which were also used as food and medicine. I've learned since that Wallace isn't the only town to hold huckleberry festivities to celebrate this delicious fare.

Leaving Wallace, we reached the lakeside hamlet of Harrison.

Fifty miles of downhill, paved, scenic, and sparsely ridden bike path later, we reached the beach on the shore of Lake Coeur d'Alene. It was ninety-something degrees, and a swim in that lake was exactly what we needed before a late lunch.

After the swim we found another unique establishment and one that was reminiscent of a café in Trempealeau, Minnesota. Just across Harrison Park, we stopped at the Cycle Haus: Bikes and Brews, which features local craft beers, German sausage, and a variety of flatbreads. Post lunch, we headed to the Harrison Creamery and Fudge Factory for more huckleberry ice cream.

Outside on a sidewalk bench, we started talking with a man our age who was wearing a bicycle brand shirt. He was interested and mentioned his wife had once done some bicycle touring. They were now vacationing in Harrison and enjoying rides on the Trail of the Coeur d'Alenes. About that time, his wife, Leslie, came over, and we started talking.

Leslie's comments were different. She didn't ask questions like others. She talked about long days in the saddle, the joy of meeting people, and the misery of heat and flat tires. She was sharing experiences, not asking questions or giving advice. At a point in the conversation, she quietly mentioned, "I did a ride like that once back in the 70s."

Pausing, I asked, "What year?"

"'76," Leslie replied.

"So, you rode the Bikecentenial?"

"Yep."

"What was it like, Leslie?"

"Amazing! I was young and sponsored by a small San Francisco newspaper to report the experience weekly. I rode a Jack Taylor bike and met some crazy and wonderful people."

"You're my hero. I wanted to ride it, but it didn't happen for me. I need your autograph," I said, chuckling.

"You must have some great stories from those weeks," I added, not sure if I was asking a question or making a statement myself.

"I do," she replied gently, with a look of recall.

I don't remember much of our conversation after that. Her

husband had wandered off, realizing, I guess, that she was the star of this show, not him. We wished each other well.

———

I began to think of our miles after leaving Harrison, Idaho, as the last phase of our journey. We continued to the terminus of the Coeur d'Alenes trail in Plummer. Turning left (south), we plunged down through Moscow and kissed the eastern flank of Washington's Palouse region. We crisscrossed the state border before snaking down Idaho's "most dangerous road" into Lewiston on the banks of the Snake River.

The Old Spiral Highway, built in 1910, drops over 2,000 feet, has over sixty hairpin turns, and distracts the motorist or cyclist with panoramic views of the Snake River's confluence with the Clearwater, where it splits the sister cities of Lewiston, Idaho, and Clarkston, Washington.

This merging of rivers essentially doubles the size of the Snake River as it flows west to blend into the Columbia at Pasco and Burbank, Washington, 125 miles to our west. We found the old highway lightly traveled, a delight on a bicycle, but it would be terrifying in a motor vehicle.

Leaving Clarkston, we soon left the banks of the Snake and headed west on Washington's Route 12. Small towns were built up every so often, separated by rural farms and open fields with crops and livestock moving across the contour of the ground. Route 12 was inevitably the neat main streets of these burgs, and it was lined with small locally owned shops on the ground floor of brick façade blocks of buildings. Each sported a unique roofline with a dedication date inscribed at the peak.

Our convergence with the Columbia River came at Wallula Junction along with the Walla Walla River, a spot of epoch-making emotional response.

Rivers are the ancient landmarks for our journey across the continent. The St. Charles in Boston; the Connecticut in Windsor Lock; the Hudson our entry to the Erie Canal corridor; the

Mohawk was colonial America's early passage into the western interior; the Mississippi, a remarkable threshold into the prairies; the Missouri, a passageway into American history and the mountains. Each of these ribbons of water was a landmark in our continental crossing.

But the Columbia was different. It would be our highway to the Pacific and journey's end. Although we would cross one more noteworthy river, the Willamette, it is the Columbia's watercourse that let us know the journey was nearly complete.

NINETEEN

Never Forget Who's Boss

Washington

Sunday, August 22, 2021: It's always darkest before the dawn. I hate this saying. For me, it speaks to a malignant resignation about your situation. Like you can't change it. Unfortunately, like many clichés, it can be accurate. We expected a hard day, but today would stand as our most challenging. Here we were, with just days until the end, and we were beaten.

If you were to check the weather for this date, you would see total sun and excellent temperatures, topography mostly flat, and then you would see the wind forecast. Mr. Wind was not about to let us off without one last notification of his malicious power. He decided today was a good day to enter from the west by southwest with a steady force of seventeen miles per hour and, often reminding us of who we were and who he was, with a knockback blow of twenty-five to thirty miles per hour.

The noise of this unceasing headwind was numbing, mind-breaking, and soul-crushing.

We tried to adapt and would think our fifty-two miles at seven-miles-per-hour average had us to Roosevelt, Washington, by 3 PM. Maybe 4 PM. We started dauntless.

The turning point to discouragement came when we hit a change in road surface from smooth, clean asphalt to rough, stone-chipped repaving with broken glass and torn tire treads everywhere. I hate to admit it, but I even tried sticking out my thumb when I saw a pickup truck coming up behind us, hoping someone would take pity. Nothing doing. If this were Ohio, someone would surely have stopped. The idea of people in the east being much nicer than these callous westerners made me even more uptight. Self-pity in any situation isn't a pretty look.

Sometime mid-day, we met Jack, a cyclist traveling east from Portland back to his home in Colorado Springs. Jack was riding a beautiful Columbine Cycles lugged steel frame bike he told me he had 175,000 miles on, a gorgeous machine. He was traveling light, a minimalist who looked like he was out for a two-hour ride, not a 1,500-mile cycle tour. He also averaged almost twenty miles per hour, with our headwind being his tailwind.

Although this route is a major thoroughfare, this area is so remote we often pedaled for ten minutes before seeing any traffic. Vehicles going in our direction were even lighter than those going east. I cannot describe the mental and physical difficulty of this day.

But, eventually, at around 5 PM, we crested a slight rise and saw the ONLY services for thirty-five miles in either direction in the tiny hamlet of Roosevelt, Washington. The Columbia River Country Store, part gas station, restaurant, camp store, and town center were thankfully open.

There were campsites out back. We planned to spend the night there, but the campground was full. The women on duty told us we could possibly pitch our tent on sloping ground behind a small tool shed if we wanted, and they would ask the manager. The wind was forecasted to continue unabated all night and most of tomorrow; we did not know what to do. Tenting here with this wind would be like sleeping next to a jackhammer as the sides flapped violently in the gale. So, we inquired about getting a ride the fifty-nine miles to The

Dalles, Oregon. The two women working the store were kind and gracious. Looking back, I can sense how frenzied I must have looked. I never asked their names, stories, or the history of this little stop along the Columbia.

It was 5:15 PM and the store was due to close at 6. The manager put out a message on her local Facebook page asking if anyone was willing to give two cyclists with bikes a ride to The Dalles before dark. I was skeptical, but Cheryl was confident.

I walked next door where I saw a firefighter's truck parked at the local mobile home park. Surely, he would pity our plight and offer to take us the hour west. He was exceptionally friendly and said he had just read the post on Facebook and would help us in a heartbeat. Except he had Covid.

Oh, well!

But in true social media fashion, by 5:45 PM, we had a ride from Mike. Mike's apparently a local legend, a former career army guy with a mysterious past. He entertained and informed us as we drove the fifty-nine miles to The Dalles, telling us about the area's history and geography. We listened politely, but I think we were so overwhelmed with relief that we would not be sleeping in a tent in punishing winds all night and cycling these exact miles tomorrow in said wind that I don't remember much of what he said.

Now, writing this, I wonder why we were so willing to jump those sixty miles without any hesitation. I could justify it by saying we needed to meet on an agreed-upon day for our friends Sam, Tyrene, and family to pick us up in Pacific City. But that could have changed. I think it is as simple as I did not want another sixty miles of thirty-five-mile-per-hour headwinds and brown-grass-laden hills as scenery. The thought of it made me even crazier than I was at the time. I tipped my helmet to Mother Nature, who, with perspicacity, was letting us know who was boss -- who would or would not allow us to dip our tires into the cold waters of the Pacific.

We felt no guilt, remorse, or self-loathing as we loaded our bikes in the pickup's bed and stepped into the massive cab of Mike's Ford F350.

And The Dalles proved to be our dawn. Our last four days on

this journey proved to be restful and refreshing, the antithesis of our miles from Umatilla to Roosevelt. We took the next day off, a need as much as a want.

TWENTY

It Just Might Happen

Oregon

Tuesday was the polar opposite of Sunday: favorable wind, bike trails in and out of towns, and other bicyclists saying hello. The amazing day ended with a 3,000-foot climb, but we were refreshed and euphoric again and enjoyed every foot.

The next morning started with a climb to Rowena Crest Overlook on the Historic Columbia Highway trail where we captured our first view of Mount Hood. The ride took us through the Twin Tunnels in Mosier and onto a welcomed downhill stretch into the neat little adventure city of Hood River.

In Hood River, we went off course and climbed steep streets to the UPS store to ship home seventeen pounds of gear between us. Then we did something we'd not done for a while: we had lunch at a great Thai restaurant before jumping on Interstate 84 for six high-traffic, white-knuckle miles. I was not sure if this was legal in Oregon, and it was orders of magnitude busier than I-90 in South Dakota, but it saved us almost 5,000 feet of elevation gain. Worth the risk.

A day later, it was crisp, clear, and all of a sudden, green. It had been weeks since we'd seen green grass and trees. It was joyful and disorienting at the same time. As we left the Best Western, we crossed under the Bridge of the Gods in Cascade Locks. This bridge also serves where the Pacific Crest Trail (PCT) crosses over the Columbia. We had now intersected America's major rivers and her three major hiking trails, the Appalachian Trail in Massachusetts, the Continental Divide Trail in Montana, and now the PCT. The morning was filled with beautiful waterfalls and wildflowers as we rambled along the Historic Columbia roadway towards Troutdale where we were to head away from the river towards Gresham and Lake Oswego.

Days moved quickly, and towns, roads, and houses passed in a blur. Starbucks, grocery stores, malls, and crisscrossing highways were all plentiful, and it reminded me of riding in Boston or Cleveland again. Climbing out of the Willamette River Valley and up our final mountain range, we passed wineries and produce farms that brought back memories of our ride through Pennsylvania on the shores of Lake Erie or our own home region along the Connecticut River. We were reminiscing now, knowing our journey across a continent was coming to a conclusion, a final milestone.

TWENTY-ONE

On the Shore of Possibility

Last miles, Friday, August 27, 2021

Leaving the Hanson House B & B in Willamina, a selfie seemed in order, but as we rode on we were both uncharacteristically quiet, pondering this whole thing, I'm sure.

The ride up through the range was nice, with narrow roads carrying very little traffic. The last twenty miles were a bonus- all downhill, no wind. So sweet.

It was on this sloping grade with an evergreen-lined brook on our right hand that Cheryl rode up next to me and matter-of-factly said, "You know, I could see us doing this again someday."

Wide-eyed, I swung my head around in her direction.

"But I want to go west to east then," she added with a smile, probably thinking about headwinds on our ride along the Columbia less than a week ago.

I mused on what greater measure of success to this whole excursion could there be but that she would consider doing it all again. So would I.

———

Soon, we rounded a bend in the road as the road lined with golden marsh grass flattened. In the distance, a large rock pillar sat between light blue sky and dark blue water. This was the sea stack off the beach at Pacific City peeking at us from three miles away.

Wildflowers again surrounded us as we rode up to the Pacific Coast Highway and Route 101 intersection, different varieties and colors than those that grew in May between the vineyards along Lake Erie, but every bit as welcome and awe-inspiring. Sitting here waiting on traffic so we could pull onto the highway, I asked Lady Google how far it was to San Francisco, knowing if I turned left instead of right, I could keep this experience alive, not wanting it to end. "Six hundred fifty-three miles," the Lady stated without much emotion or recognition of what she had just been a part of.

How do you describe this moment? Pictorially, we were separated and all alone on a very, very crowded beach where hundreds of people were enjoying a sun-washed day in the water, climbing the dunes, and eating at a seaside brewery. They did not notice us crossing a wide swath of sand, pushing our front tires toward the Pacific Ocean, completing a picture, the first half of which had our back tires in Boston's Atlantic.

Cheryl cried, almost whispering, "I can't believe we did this. I can't believe it's over." She had never set out to cross a continent with me. It was my dream, and she came along lovingly and supportively. But at the Mississippi, on the brink of mid-ride, she committed to sticking it out.

"Did I really do this, or is this just a dream?" she added

I was numb, unbelieving that success had been realized. I looked around and simultaneously wanted to tell everyone around us what we were doing there and why, while being extremely happy that it was just the two of us and we could relish it together. At that moment, no one else could comprehend it all.

As people of faith, our overwhelming sensation was gratitude for the divine goodness we knew enabled hope and dreams—dreams delayed, perhaps, surely not denied.

As we were walking out of the surf, a couple approached and asked if we'd like them to take our picture. They knew.

Today, I am sorry I can't remember their names. I remember how kind they were, how they shared that they, too, were cyclists, and they were in Pacific City to celebrate their sixty-fifth wedding anniversary. It was not lost on us that they were married the year I was born. Another omen like Kris had proffered three weeks ago on our last day in Montana? Angels visiting us unaware in this moment? Coincidence? No, I know it was not a coincidence.

I stood on the beach and thought about how to process this ride. Like adolescents, we rode the Erie Canal, not exactly sure of what we were doing or going to do next. Leaving Buffalo was like entering the time when you build, learn, and grow in life. The decades before mid-life where disenchantment threatens. We left the stark dryness of South Dakota like leaving the angst of mid-life. Wyoming to Missoula was a period of freshness and pleasant roads followed by hitting the walls of disappointment and unfulfilled wishes. The unexpected opportunity to start again, getting back on the road to experience synchronicity, renewal, and altered visions of possibility. It was all a metaphor for our life.

So now what?

I thought about our youngest granddaughter, Gwyneth. She was four years and six months old; I was sixty-four years old. Both of us stood on the shore of a phase of life. She at the first; I at the last.

Both of us faced a wide-open sea, a horizon of possibilities.

Acknowledgments

As a man of faith and disciple of Jesus, my first acknowledgment is of His divine goodness, which allowed us to embark on and complete this ride. I am exceptionally grateful.

Cheryl's confidence in me in everything is more than anyone understands or I could describe. Riding all the miles together made the journey across the continent and life most sweet. Our family took an interest in and encouraged us every day. That is enormous support that adds joy and purpose to life. To quote Nora Gibbons McBrierty, "You're a great bunch, all of ya."

Betsy Hany, Colleen Luginbuhl, Ken Luginbuhl, Cheryl Morgan, Chris Putur, and Katie Zahner did the tough work, giving me feedback, artwork, and proofreading, all with kindness. This smoothed the rough edges and provided ideas that improved the final version of this book.

Warren Zahner kicked all this off with his uncharacteristically quick reply, "We can make that happen." I miss our rides, tours, and talks. I am deeply grateful for our friendship.

My editor, Adria Carey Perez, is directly responsible for the professionalism in this book. She added competence above my skill and know-how without taking away my voice. Adria's guidance made the good parts into the best pages; the poor parts were cut with directness and reason, and the places of promise turned memorable.